THE INSTRUCTION OF PHILOSOPHY AND PSYCHOANALYSIS BY TRAGEDY

Jacques Lacan and Gabriel Marcel
Read
Paul Claudel

Ann Bugliani

THE INSTRUCTION OF PHILOSOPHY AND PSYCHOANALYSIS BY TRAGEDY

Jacques Lacan and Gabriel Marcel
Read
Paul Claudel

Ann Bugliani

International Scholars Publications
San Francisco - London - Bethesda
1999

Library of Congress Cataloging-in-Publication Data

Bugliani, Ann.
    The instruction of philosophy and psychoanalysis by tragedy : Jacques
Lacan and Gabriel Marcel read Paul Claudel / Ann Bugliani.
        p. cm.
    Includes bibliographical references and index.
    ISBN 1-57309-308-4 -- ISBN 1-57309-307-6(pbk.).
    1. Claudel, Paul, 1868-1955--Criticism and interpretation. 2. Lacan,
Jacques, 1901- . 3. Marcel, Gabriel, 1843-1909. 4. Psychoanalysis in
literature. 5. Philosophy in literature. 6. Tragedy. I. Title.
PQ2605.L2Z5963 1998   98-30393
848'.91209--dc21   CIP

Copyright 1999 by Ann Bugliani.

Editorial Inquiries:
International Scholars Publications
7831 Woodmont Avenue, #345
Bethesda, MD 20814
website: www.interscholars.com
To order: (800) 55-PUBLISH

ad maiorem Dei gloriam

TABLE OF CONTENTS

ABBREVIATIONS

A	Kowsar, "Lacan's *Antigone*"
B	Bugliani, *Women and the Feminine Principle in the Works of Paul Claudel*
BS	Raymond, *De Baudelaire au Surréalisme*
C	Gellrich, *Tragedy and Theatre: The Problem of Conflict Since Aristotle*
Cs	Girard, *Critiques dans un souterrain*
CV	Moraly, "Claudel Voyant"
D	Derrida, *Dissemination*
E	Lacan, *L'éthique de la psychanalyse*
Edu	Moran, *Gabriel Marcel: Existentialist, Philosopher, Dramatist, Educator*
Ex	Troisfontaines, *De l'existence à l'être*
F	Nussbaum, *The Fragility of Goodness*
Fr	Ricoeur, *Freud and Philosophy*
IT	Marcel, "Influence du Théâtre"
J	Claudel, *Journal*
LP	Edmundson, *Literature Against Philosophy, Plato to Derrida*
LTD	Wyschogrod, et al., eds, *Lacan and Theological Discourse*
Mal	Davignon, *Le Mal chez Gabriel Marcel*
Mass	Marcel, *Man Against Mass Society*
Mr	Girard, *Mensonge romantique et vérité romanesque*
N	Sallis, *Crossings: Nietzsche and the Space of Tragedy*
Oc	Claudel, *Oeuvres complètes*
One	Ricoeur, *Oneself As Another*
Op	Claudel, *Oeuvre poétique*
Opr	Claudel, *Oeuvres en prose*
Pc	Tilliette, *Philosophes contemporains*
PE	Marcel, *The Philosophy of Existence*
PGM	Gallagher, *The Philosophy of Gabriel Marcel*
PLT	Heidegger, *Poetry, Language, Thought*
R	Marcel, *Tragic Wisdom and Beyond Including Conversations Between Paul Ricoeur and Gabriel Marcel*
Reg	Marcel, *Regards sur le théâtre de Paul Claudel*
S	Ricoeur, *The Symbolism of Evil*

ACKNOWLEDGMENTS

I would like to gratefully acknowledge the support I have received from Loyola University Chicago for this study. This support included an administrative leave, a semester as an Ethics Fellow at Loyola's Center for Ethics, and a summer research grant. I also want to thank colleagues at the various conferences here and abroad where I have read drafts of portions of Chapters 2, 3, 4, 5, 6, and 7. Their remarks have been helpful and encouraging. I am also grateful to Professor Susan Cavallo and Dr. Americo Bugliani for reading the manuscript and for their many useful suggestions.

Portions of chapter 2 appeared in *Paul Claudel: les Odes,* Sergio Villani, ed., Woodbridge, Ontario: Les Editions Albion, 1994, in French.

INTRODUCTION

In this study I explore the intersection of tragedy and, more broadly, literature with philosophy, ethics, and psychoanalysis. The object of this exploration is three-fold: to examine the tension between philosophy and literature, to bring to light the extraordinary teaching of tragedy, and to demonstrate the manner in which some of the foremost contemporary figures in philosophy, ethics, and psychoanalysis defer to that teaching, particularly as it is found in the works of Paul Claudel, considered by many to be the greatest poet and dramatist of twentieth century France. Through my work I hope to further the interdisciplinary conversation and perhaps stimulate it by reminding us that literary theory is important because literature is important. It should help us refocus on the primacy of literature. It should also serve to acquaint an English-speaking readership with the works of Paul Claudel. Jacques Lacan and Gabriel Marcel are well known and widely recognized for their contributions to western thought, yet Paul Claudel, whose instruction they each acknowledge, is relatively unknown.

I begin my study with the first famous detractor of art and drama—Plato. I consider his banishment of the poets and the many reasons for it, highlighting his desire for rational self-sufficiency which results in an effort to repudiate all elements which are deemed irrational or uncontrollable, an effort repeated throughout the history of Western thought. I interpret this repudiation as an attempt to silence the gods—since the poets are their mouthpieces—and to veil certain subversive truths. Finally, I also examine the feminine character of the metaphors used in connection with what has been scapegoated, and the link between the feminine and the deity.

I then proceed to introduce the reader to Paul Claudel drawing a parallel between Plato's misgivings concerning poetic inspiration and Claudel's. Claudel, too, saw the dangers in abandonment to his muse. He, too, feared death and desired rational self-sufficiency and mastery. These fears and desires are laid bare in his great ode, "La Muse qui est la Grâce" ("The Muse Who Is Grace") which I analyze in Chapter 2. I point to the fact that despite his fears and desire, Claudel yielded to poetic inspiration and, as a result, had access to a certain wisdom, a tragic wisdom, which will be explored by Jacques Lacan and Gabriel Marcel.

I begin considering what tragedy teaches in Chapter 3 by examining its relation to ethics and psychoanalysis. In Plato's view tragic poems could never be good teachers of ethical wisdom because they indulge the irrational nature which has no discernment. In contrast, Aristotle has a high regard for tragedy. He gives it a place of honor in his discussion of the education of the young. Here I consider Martha Nussbaum's thesis that for Aristotle the viewing of pitiable and fearful things in tragedy, *and* our responses of pity and fear themselves, can serve to teach us something of importance. For Aristotle, the function of tragedy is to accomplish, through these emotions, a clarification, illumination or catharsis thus contributing to human self-understanding. Note is also taken of the tendency in the Anglo-American tradition, which Nussbaum discusses, to assume that the ethical text should, in the process of inquiry, converse with the intellect alone. The claim is often made in this tradition that the human being's relation to value in the world is not, or should not be, profoundly tragic. This is in marked contrast with what one finds in much of the continental tradition which I examine in this book.

For Nietzsche, tragedy is the natural healing power against the Dionysian abyss. Paul Ricoeur contends that catharsis, or the metaphorization of terror and pity, is, in fact, the condition for all properly ethical instruction. He affirms that tragedy teaches us the inevitable place of conflict in moral life, refusing to offer solutions, yet outlining a wisdom capable of directing us in conflicts. A consideration of Ricoeur's thought opens the broader question of literature, or narrativity, in general, which he believes serves as a propaedeutic to ethics. It also leads me to a discussion of psychoanalysis through consideration of his views on the relation of dreams to the creation of works of art.

I conclude this chapter by addressing the thought of René Girard who asserts that there exists in certain literary works a knowledge concerning desire which is superior to anything that has ever been proposed by psychology or psychoanalysis. Girard suggests that the scientific pretensions which have dominated three quarters of the twentieth century may in the end be shown to be disappointing and deceptive. He advocates retrieving what failing dogmatisms have disdained, the great literary masterpieces.

Jacques Lacan, as we know, gives great heed to the instruction of tragedy. In his seminar on the transference stage in psychoanalytic therapy which took place in 1960-1961, but was published in France in 1991, he tells us that he was forced to turn to tragedy, as Freud was, to make himself understood. In 1958 his focus was *Hamlet*. The following year he examined the significance of ancient tragedy by studying *Antigone*. Here, in *Le transfert*, he speaks of exploring contemporary experience in search of an exemplar of human desire which would serve to illustrate his thought, arguing that Freud's insights could not possibly have emerged by happenstance, in isolation. Lacan finds his exemplar of modern tragedy in Paul Claudel's Coûfontaine trilogy—*The Hostage*, *Hard Bread*, and *The Humiliated Father*. He is convinced that Paul Claudel is one of the greatest poets who has ever lived and that his entire theatre is, indeed, *the* tragedy of desire. Chapter 4 contains an exposition of Lacan's analysis of these three plays. In *The Hostage*, Lacan contends Claudel goes beyond the terror and pity of the ancients and even beyond Job's sufferings and resignation. Lacan sustains that in this play we have the sign that a new meaning has been given to human tragedy. A discussion ensues of why all prior extremes of suffering have been surpassed by modernity. In *Hard Bread*, Lacan analyzes the theme of the father and claims, once again, that all norms are bypassed. We see an extreme derision of the father figure verging on the abject in this play. Here, Lacan particularly admires Claudel's creative reworking of the Oedipus complex which he believes confirms Freud's discoveries and proves that Freud was right about the Oedipus complex. In *The Humiliated Father*, Lacan asserts that Claudel shows us what becomes of desire made visible in the form of a woman. Lacan also reviews the structuralist articulation of myth in an attempt to determine of what use Claudel's theory of myth is. Lacan's treatment of Claudel highlights the originality of Claudel's tragic wisdom which Lacan mines for instruction and confirmation of psychoanalytic theories.

Gabriel Marcel, in addition to being one of the foremost philosophers of the twentieth century, was also a critic, an accomplished musician, and a playwright of note. Though Sartre characterized him as an existentialist in his essay "The Humanism of Existentialism," Marcel eventually repudiated this label, preferring to identify his thought as neo-Socratic. In his work, which is analyzed in Chapter 5, reflection is almost always linked to experience of the most concrete kind. He repudiated what he calls "the spirit of abstraction" for precisely the reasons considered in Chapter 1—it lies about the nature of the human condition. In fact, the basic characteristic of his philosophy was to dispute the validity of the pretensions of totalizing thought. The moment we have a system, he says, we are concerned with exploiting and managing it. Marcel is instead concerned with the universal to be found in the depth of experience, the kind of experience in which one is personally involved and in which something is at stake. He believed that the natural trend of philosophy leads it into a sphere where it seems that tragedy has simply vanished— evaporated at the touch of abstract thought. Abstraction makes it impossible not only to find a response to tragedy, to evil, to suffering and to death, but even to really consider or envisage them. Plato's gesture is repeated and the tragic factors of human existence are banished to some disreputable suburb of thought—to literature. For Marcel, any philosophy that seeks to elude or side-step the themes of death, despair, and betrayal is guilty of the worst betrayal imaginable. The only wisdom possible is a tragic wisdom which is less a state than a goal and whose victory is not over insecurity itself, but over the anguish which seems to be its inevitable consequence. I conclude this chapter with Emmanuel Levinas' assessment of Marcel's contribution to thought.

In Chapter 6 I explore the nature of dramatic creation in an effort to understand its fecundity, its relation to thought, and its link to the transcendent. I begin with Marcel's views. For him, the connection between philosophy and drama was the most intimate possible. In fact, he claims that his philosophy is existential to the degree that it is simultaneously drama, that is, dramatic creation. I then analyze a Claudelian text on dramatic creation from which I draw parallels with both Marcel's thought and Martin Heidegger's.

Returning to Marcel in Chapter 7, I point to his recognition of music and poetry as perhaps the most appropriate vehicles for the expression of the universal. As Stephen Jolin, his translator, points out, his advice to the philosopher dedicated to the true spirit of universality is to pay attention to music and poetry, to Mozart and to Claudel. Marcel, one of the most original of contemporary thinkers, freely admits that Claudel's influence on him was profound. In Claudel, Marcel sees not only one of the greatest poets of all times, but also one of the most complete and disconcerting artistic personalities. He believes Claudel's theatre represents a revolution without precedent in France. It is in opposition to the whole French dramatic tradition. Neither psychological, nor social or critical; Marcel characterizes it instead as cosmic or ontological—a theatre in which something essential is always at stake. Marcel finds Claudel's early plays remarkable for their portrayal of the human condition, particularly *Tête d'Or* and *The City* which were written at a time when in France, and even in Germany, existential thought had not yet become conscious of itself,. He claims they announce all of French existential philosophy in the global, tragic awareness of the modern world they contain. However, as this world view with its principle of destruction disappears in Claudel's later plays, it will be replaced by what Marcel calls a dogmatism which he believes is tied to Claudel's ascent in the world, to his success and prominence. Claudel becomes an important personage and, in a certain way, the prisoner of this very importance. He moves from tragedy to drama, a shift Marcel considers disastrous. For Marcel, wisdom today can only be tragic.

I end my study by considering the prophetic phenomenon which Marcel, among others, discerns in Claudel's early plays. An examination of this phenomenon leads back to one of the central themes of our exploration: the desire for rational mastery, the will to power, and its relation to inspiration and creativity. In other words, to conclude I revisit Plato's banishment of the poets and the tension between philosophy and literature. I then consider Kenneth Gallagher's reflections on creativity and I join him in affirming that if anything can, the artistic process should demonstrate that the creative self is not an autonomous subject. It is the nature of this process which accounts for the instruction of philosophy and psychoanalysis by tragedy.

CHAPTER 1

SILENCING THE GODS

In the *Ion*[1] Plato asserts that all good poets compose their poems and plays, not by art, but because they are inspired or possessed. A poet is a light, winged, holy thing and there is no invention in him until he has been inspired and is out of his senses, until his mind is no longer in him. His words are uttered in a state of unconsciousness. When he has not attained that state he is powerless and unable to utter his oracles. It is the muse who impels them; it is god who uses him as a minister or mouthpiece; god himself is the speaker. The divine power at work functions like a magnet which not only attracts but also imparts to those attracted a power to attract others in turn. Inspiration is communicated from god to the poet; from the poet to the actors; and then, through the actors, god sways the souls of men. In the *Phaedrus* (244-45) Plato speaks of this again when he explains that there are three kinds of madness. The first is simply an evil; the second, the madness of prophecy, is a divine gift and the source of the best blessings granted to men. It is averred that the prophetess at Delphi, for instance, when out of her senses, conferred great benefits on Hellas, but when in her senses, few or none. The third kind is the madness of those possessed by the muses who take hold of a soul, inspiring frenzy and awakening lyrical measures and, with these, adorning the myriad actions of ancient heroes for the instruction of posterity.

The poems and plays of antiquity were then the inspired texts, the scriptures

---

[1]Plato, *The Dialogues of Plato*, trans. Benjamin Jowett (Chicago: William Benton, 1952), 533-36.

from which theological and ethical principles were drawn. Yet sacred as these texts were, they were not immune from critical examination and so we note that when Plato turns to the oracles for principles of theology in the *Republic* (II 376-III 404), he is disturbed by the representation of the gods he finds in Homer and Aeschylus.

Reason and logic teach that god is perfectly simple and true both in word and deed. He does not deceive either by sign or word, by dream or waking vision. Furthermore, it is impossible that he should ever be willing to change; every god remains absolutely and forever in his own form. The great poets are then guilty of misrepresenting the nature of gods and heroes when they depict wars in heaven and heroes in conflict with their friends and relatives. Plato contends that in the well-ordered state children should be taught that arguing is unholy and that there have never been any quarrels among citizens, much less among the gods. The poets or narrators should not suggest anything to the contrary, nor should they suggest that the wicked are often happy, the good miserable, or injustice profitable when undetected. The claim that the gods could be the author of evil is also to be strenuously denied. Indeed, god, being good, could only be the author of the good. The tales the young hear should be models of virtuous thoughts. Through them, they are to be taught to honor the gods, to honor their parents and to value friendship with one another. The young must be temperate, obedient, and able to exercise self-control in sensual pleasures. Tales of vice, conflict and disorder can only have a bad effect, for everyone begins to excuse his own vices when he is convinced that similar wickedness is always being perpetrated by no less than "the relatives of Zeus." As for the guardians of the state, they should, as far as possible, be true worshipers of the gods and like them. They must be courageous men who will choose death in battle rather than defeat and slavery. Yet will anyone choose death who believes the world below to be as it is depicted by Homer—real and terrible? Poetry is then deemed dangerous and its dangers are due to its very nature.

Plato tells us that all mythology and poetry is a narration of events, either past, present, or to come and all narration may be either simple narration, imitation, or a union of the two. In simple narration, the poet speaks in his own person, never leading us to suppose he is anyone else. In imitation, he speaks in the person of another, assimilating himself to another, imitating the person whose character he assumes. Tragedy and comedy are both wholly mimetic, whereas the epic combines both simple narration and imitation. We also learn that there is one sort of style for the virtuous and another for the unscrupulous. Harmony and discord flow naturally from style, and beauty of style, grace, and good rhythm depend on simplicity—the true simplicity of a rightly and nobly ordered mind and character. The style of the virtuous is narrative with the admixture of very little imitation. It is simple; it has few changes and therefore has a single harmony and rhythm. The unscrupulous, on the other hand, will imitate anything and so they require all sorts of harmonies and rhythms because there are all sorts of changes. Just as complexity in food brings disease, in style it engenders license. Simplicity, on the other hand, produces temperance in the soul. In Plato's state one man plays one part only, because human nature is not twofold or manifold. As Michelle Gellrich notes in *Tragedy and Theatre: The Problems of Conflict Since Aristotle*[2] in his state there is to be no fragmentation of the singularity and unity of *ethos* essential to the natural division of labor, according to which each person performs the activity that most suits him by temperament and training. The guardians, for instance, are to dedicate themselves wholly to the maintenance of freedom in the state. They ought not to practice or imitate anything else. If they imitate at all, it should be those who are courageous, temperate, holy, and free. They should not depict or imitate any illiberality or baseness, lest from imitation they should come to be what they imitate, for imitation can grow into habits and become second nature. As Gellrich rightly concludes, for Plato social order is shaken by mimesis which destroys the principle of differentiation essential to the hierarchy of the state.

Plato pursues this theme again in Book X (595-608). Here, he states

---

[2]Michelle Gellrich, *Tragedy and Theatre: The Problem of Conflict Since Aristotle* (Princeton: Princeton University Press, 1988), 100. Henceforth cited as *C*.

categorically that all poetical imitations are ruinous to the understanding of the hearers. The tragic poet is an imitator and, like all other imitators, he is thrice removed from the truth, third in descent from nature. First is the idea, form, or essence created by god; second is the particular, the appearance of reality; third is the imitation of that appearance. After establishing this hierarchy, Plato proceeds to attack Homer as the captain and teacher of all the tragedians. What state, he asks, was ever governed by Homer's help? Was any war carried on successfully by him? If he never did any public service, was he privately a guide or teacher of any? If Homer had possessed knowledge and not been a mere imitator, if he had really been able to educate and improve mankind, can it be imagined that he would not have had many followers? Plato concludes that all poets, including Homer, are mere imitators, who copy images of virtue, but never reach the truth. Imitation is only a kind of play or sport and the tragic poets are imitators in the highest degree. In the *Phaedrus* (248) we learn that the soul which has seen the most truth will come to birth as a philosopher, as an artist, or as someone with a musical and loving nature; the one which has seen truth in the second degree will be a righteous king or warrior chief; the soul which is of the third class will be a politician, or economist, or trader; the fourth will be a lover of gymnastic toils, or a physician; the fifth will lead the life of a prophet or hierophant; to the sixth will be assigned the character of a poet or some other imitative artist; to the seventh the life of an artisan or husbandman; to the eighth that of a sophist or demagogue; and to the ninth, that of a tyrant.

Plato reasons that just as imitation is far removed from truth, the principle within us which is its accomplice is equally removed from reason and has no true or healthy aim. Imitative art is an inferior who attracts and marries an inferior in us and engenders inferior offspring. Man has two distinct principles in him; one higher, the other lower. It is the lower, rebellious principle which furnishes a great variety of material for imitation. The wise and calm temperament, being always nearly equable, is not easy to imitate or to appreciate when imitated especially by a promiscuous crowd in a theatre. The art of the imitative poet who aims at being popular, is not intended to please or to affect the higher rational principle in the soul. The imitative poet imparts an evil constitution to the soul, for he indulges the irrational nature which has no discernment. He is but a manufacturer of images and is very far removed from the truth. It is only the powers of calculation and measurement which the soul possesses that allow it to pierce appearances, the illusions of the senses, and arrive at the truth. It is then the better part of the soul that trusts to measure and calculation. It is the inferior principles of the soul which are opposed to them.

But there is more. Poetry also has the power of actually harming the good, for even the best of us delight in giving way to sympathy when we listen to a passage of Homer in which he represents some pitiful hero who laments his sorrows. In fact, we are in raptures at the excellence of the poet who stirs our feelings most. Yet, in real life, when sorrow strikes we pride ourselves on the opposite quality of calm and patience.

Plato considers the value of catharsis when he asks if it could not be said that the natural desire to relieve our sorrow by weeping and lamentation, which is kept under control in our own calamities, is satisfied by the poets when we allow the sympathetic element to break loose because the sorrow is another's. Many claim that there can be no disgrace in this; but he warns that few realize that from the evil of others something is communicated to ourselves. And so, the feeling of sorrow which has gathered strength at the sight of the misfortunes of others is with difficulty repressed in our own afflictions. The same holds true of the ridiculous, or of lust and anger, or desire, pain, and pleasure. Poetry feeds and waters the passions instead of drying them up. She lets them rule although they ought to be controlled if mankind is ever to increase in happiness and virtue.

To those who say that Homer was the educator of Hellas and that he is useful for education and for the ordering of human things, and indeed that one's whole life should be regulated according to him, Plato responds by acknowledging that Homer is the greatest of poets and the first of the tragedians, but he remains firm in his conviction that he is dangerous. In fact, hymns to the gods and praises of famous men are the only poetry which he would admit into his state. The imitative poet is to be exiled from the well-ordered commonwealth because he awakens, nourishes, and strengthens the feelings while impairing reason. The consequence of allowing either epic or lyric verse is that neither law nor reason will be the rulers in the state but instead pleasure and pain.

Plato concludes his remarks by recalling the ancient enmity between philosophy and poetry. Fearing the accusation of harshness, he admits that he is very conscious of poetry's feminine charms. Poetry might even be permitted to return from exile if her defenders can show that she is not only pleasant but also useful to the state and to human life. If this can be proved, he surmises that we shall surely be the gainers. If not, like others who are enamored of something, but restrain themselves when their desires oppose their interests, so too must we give poetry up, but not without a struggle. For Plato, like all others, is inspired by the love of poetry implanted in him by the education of a noble state.

In any case, poetry is not to be regarded as seriously attaining to the truth and those who listen to her should be on guard against her seductions. For much is at stake—whether we are to be good or bad—and what will any one be profited if under the influence of honor, or money, or power, or poetry, we neglect justice and virtue.

As we consider Plato's conclusions, we are struck by a number of things. First, and most apparent, are the contradictions. Repeated assertions that the poets are divinely inspired contrast with the attack on poetry and leave one to wonder what really is to be banished in the state. Is all inspiration to be quenched and are the gods themselves to be silenced? Do they become the scapegoats which are expelled in the interest of rationality and control?

We have seen that claims are made that the poets are merely mouthpieces for the gods; yet there are also claims that they misrepresent the gods, particularly concerning conflict. The gods and heroes are not in conflict, nor can they ever be, or so Plato would have children believe. Apparently, the poets' truth, which comes from the gods, is too subversive of order to be allowed. Is it the truth itself then, or certain truths—concerning violence and conflict, for instance—which are suppressed at the very dawn of philosophical thought? Gellrich points to Plato's consistently negative tenor toward conflict, whether psychological, social, or metaphysical. The fact that Plato's early life coincided with the disastrous years of the Peloponnesian War, the shattering of the Athenian Empire, and the fierce civil strife of oligarchs and democrats in the years of anarchy 404-403 BC may in part account for these attitudes, but we must also remember the reasons for the impulse to deny the role of violence in society unveiled by René Girard.[3]

Paralyzing fears are at work here; fears so great that they lead to the sacrifice of inspiration, passion and pleasure. As Jacques Derrida observes in *Plato's Pharmacy*[4] the price that must be paid for rational mastery is the death of the body, the renunciation of passion and pleasure. Derrida says that it is the child in the man that is afraid. The little boy within fears death; and the remedy, the antidote, or exorcism Socrates recommends for this fear is dialectics—training in dialectics, to seek to know oneself through mutual questioning and self-examination. (*D* 121) Self-knowledge and self-mastery are the best forms of exorcism that can be applied against the terrors of the child faced with death. According to Derrida, philosophy consists of offering reassurance to children. That is, if one prefers, of taking them out of childhood, of forgetting about the child, or, inversely, but by the same token, of speaking first and foremost for that little boy within, of teaching him to speak—to dialogue—by displacing his fear or his desire. (*D* 122) The order of knowledge is not the transparent order of forms and ideas, as one might be tempted retrospectively to interpret it; it is instead the antidote. Truth, law, knowledge, dialectics, philosophy—all these are other names for that *pharmakon* or remedy that must be opposed to the bewitching fear of death. (*D* 124) It might also be said that what is feared is that excessive momentum that entrains being into the simulacrum, the mask,

---

[3]See René Girard, *Des choses cachées depuis la fondation du monde* (Paris: Grasset, 1978).

[4]Jacques Derrida, "Plato's Pharmacy," *Dissemination*, trans. Barbara Johnson (Chicago: University of Chicago Press, 1981), 120. Henceforth cited as *D*.

the festival, play, and that there can be no antidote but that which enables one to remain measured. (*D* 140)   The impulse is then to substitute *logos* for myth, discourse for theater, demonstration for illustration. (*D* 142)

In discussing the role of the banished scapegoat in antiquity, J. P. Vernant says that in the person of the ostracized, the city expels what in it is too elevated, what incarnates the evil which can come to it from above.   In the evil of the *pharmakos*, it expels what is vilest in itself, what incarnates the evil that menaces it from below.   By this double and complementary rejection the city delimits itself in relation to what is not yet known and what transcends the known: it takes the proper measure of the human in opposition on one side to the divine and heroic, on the other to the bestial and monstrous.[5]   Poetry, as we have seen, is thought to have this dual nature. It draws from what is lowest and what is highest in man.   Plato speaks of the irrationality of poetry and inspiration, its uncontrollable spellbinding powers of enchantment, its mesmerizing fascination, in other words, its lower functions; yet, he also speaks of its divine origin.   Philosophical or dialectical mastery offers protection not only from the fear of death but also from all uncontrolled and uncontrollable bewitching influences.   Platonism, the dominant structure of the history of metaphysics which sets up the whole of western metaphysics in its conceptuality is, Derrida tells us, the most powerful effort at this mastery.   We conclude then that poetry is banished and the voice of the gods is silenced so that man might gain rational self-sufficiency and control of himself and his environment.

In discussing the Platonic scene Derrida makes much of the family metaphors he finds in it concerning fathers and sons.   The voice of the gods which must be silenced is, in fact, the father's voice.   Derrida tells us that nothing is said of the mother in these family metaphors and, although that is true, we must insist on the importance of the metaphors of femininity, overlooked by Derrida in his *Pharmacy*, but to which we now turn our attention.   It would seem that the voice of the gods, the father's voice, is mediated to us through the feminine.   This is indeed corroborated

[5]J. P. Vernant, "Ambiguity and Reversal: On the Enigmatic Structure of *Oedipus Rex*, " *New Literary History* 10, no. 3 (1978): 491-92. Cited in *D* 131.

by other ancient texts.

In a Hebrew text predating Plato by several hundred years, Sophia, or divine wisdom, says that she is the inventor of lucidity of thought and that her mouth proclaims the truth. In her are found good advice, sound judgement, perception, and strength. She tells us that Yahweh created her when his purpose first unfolded, before the oldest of his works, and then she adds:

> I was by his side, a master craftsman, delighting him day after day,
>
> ever at play in his presence, at play everywhere in this world,
>
> delighting to be with the sons of men.[6]

These lofty valuations of femininity clearly contrast, however, with what we find in Plato. But it is not surprising that in a society in which boys replace women as the object of desire, the feminine should be condemned as a debasing influence, particularly the playful, beguiling feminine of poetry which Plato fears will subvert the order of his city.

The Hebrew text is also interesting because it identifiesthe feminine with the very intellectual powers in the interests of which the feminine is sacrificed in the Greek text. Even more interesting is the fact that the same identification may be found in Plato. In the *Sophist* (259) and the *Statesman* (281), the art of weaving, which is clearly feminine[7], serves as an analogy for the art of discerning, or the dialectic, which is an art of purification and protection used to remove evil from the soul. Division, which may also be called discerning, is followed by composition, or the union of conceptions with one another, through which we attain to the discourse of reason. Thus in weaving, the separation of the clotted and matted fibers is followed by the spinning of a firm thread called the warp, and of a looser, softer one called the woof. The art of entwining warp and woof is the art of . The royal web is woven by a queenly power able to join the opposites. The art of dialectic is then described by a "metaphor" borrowed from the order of the very thing to be excluded

---

[6]Proverbs 8:30-31

[7]Homer represents the Moirai as spinners. They are mighty goddesses who dispense the inevitable.

and overcome—the order of the feminine.

Freud, too, had something to say concerning weaving, corroborating the intuition of femininity. In his lecture on the "Psychology of Women"[8] he sets out to enumerate the mental characteristics of mature femininity. Among these he cites a greater amount of narcissism, which is why women need to be loved more than to love; vanity, which results from penis-envy; modesty, originally designed to hide the deficiency of their genitals; and envy, due to the inadequacy of their sense of justice since the demands of justice modify envy, laying down the conditions under which one is willing to part with it. Although women contributed but little to the discoveries and inventions of civilization, there is perhaps one technical process that they did discover—that of plaiting and weaving. Freud guesses at the unconscious motive behind this achievement:

> Nature herself might be regarded as having provided a model for
> imitation by causing pubic hair to grow at the period of sexual
> maturity so as to veil the genitals. The step that remained to be taken
> was to attach the hairs permanently together, whereas in the body
> they are fixed in the skin and only tangled with one another.

Imagining the reaction of his audience to these remarks, he adds:

> If you repudiate this idea as being fantastic, and accuse me of having
> an *idée fixe* on the influence exercised by the lack of a penis upon the
> development of femininity, I cannot of course defend myself.

He then admits that his observations are incomplete and fragmentary and concludes by saying:

> If you want to know more about femininity you must interrogate your
> own experience or turn to the poets, or else wait until science can give
> you more profound and more coherent information. (*W* 864)

What is significant here is, of course, both the remarks concerning weaving and the reference to poetry. It is indeed through the inspiration of poetry that certain truths

---

[8]Sigmund Freud, "Psychology of Women," *New Lectures in Psycho-Analysis* (Chicago: William Benton, 1952), 862. Henceforth cited as *W*.

concerning emotions and feeling, passion and desire—all of which are somehow thought to be womanly—can be found.

CHAPTER 2

READING PAUL CLAUDEL

Paul Claudel had much to say about the creative process and it is fascinating to note that he agreed in great measure with Plato. He had serious misgivings concerning poetic inspiration. He, too, felt that inspiration was inimitable and that no amount of talent or artifice could possibly replace it. Yet, he also warns of its dangers, dangers which some poets underestimated—Rimbaud, for instance, or Hugo whom he characterizes as an unquestionably inspired poet who did not sufficiently mistrust his inspirations.[1]

What follows is a reading of one of Claudel's *Five Great Odes*, "La Muse qui est la Grâce" ("The Muse Who Is Grace")[2] which will illustrate the degree to which the dangers discerned by Plato were indeed encountered by Claudel.[3]

---

[1]Paul Claudel, *Oeuvres en prose*, Bibliothèque de la Pléiade (Paris: Gallimard, 1965), 474. Henceforth cited as *Opr*.

[2]Paul Claudel, "La Muse qui est la Grâce," *Oeuvre poétique*, Bibliothèque de la Pléiade (Paris: Gallimard, 1967), 263-77. Henceforth cited as *Op*.

[3]This reading was originally published in French as "'O la femme qui est en moi': Paul Claudel et 'La Muse qui est la Grâce,'" *Paul Claudel: les Odes* (Woodbridge, Ont: Les Editions Albion, 1994), 187-200. Translation mine.

The Muse Who is Grace

The very first image in this ode likens the poet to a ship or galley lifted by the sea at the tide of syzygy. Then, still in the same verse, the poet becomes a thoroughbred. The sea undoubtedly represents his inspiration or his muse. She returns to him on the occasion of the syzygy which is at once the conjunction and the opposition of the sun and the moon, that is, of masculine and feminine principles. But his muse is also the Amazon, or female warrior, that jumps on the huge thoroughbred and brutally seizes its reins with a burst of laughter. This first verse contains all the fundamental ambiguity that characterizes the entire ode. The syzygy, which simultaneously implies conjunction and opposition, is the sign of it.

The sea, also essentially feminine, brings liberty. She raises the poet with her swelling and provokes in him a frenetic movement compared to a dance. But she also carries him along by her currents. The Amazon wants to subjugate him by brutally seizing his reins with a burst of laughter. Clearly, the poet does not control either his inspiration or his muse. He will, at first, join her, then resist her.

Everything happens at night, in silence. The night itself, like the sea, is yet another image of the muse who returns to seek him out. And because of her coming, the poet will at last be able to be himself. He is tired of the role he plays among men. A window opens and the conjunction, the communication, takes place. The poet will henceforth identify himself completely with this woman within him. He will compare himself to a young girl at the window of a beautiful white moonlit castle who awaits the sound of two horses. The chasm of night is like a room lit bright for the young girl at her first dance.

When the intoxication overtakes him, he is at the mercy of the gods. He hears a voice within him, a stirring of joy, the arousal of the Olympic cohort. Now, all the men for whom he plays a role matter little. It is not for them that he was made, but rather for the rapture of this sacred measure. Under the influence of his inspiration he has the courage to brave the opinion of others. When the great poetic wing unfurls, only rhythm counts. What does it matter whether men follow him or not, whether they understand or not? He only wants to put on the golden sandals. And then everything is transformed—words, sentences, flowers, even his feet, for now he walks on water. Now he treads on that very sea that had lifted him, shakened him, carried him along. Now it is he that holds the reins of his inspiration and the dialogue can begin.

Stanza I

In the exchange that follows one can discern what characterizes the relationship between the poet and his muse whom he addresses in this stanza. He is clearly engaged in a power struggle with her, as we saw in the introduction. He pleads: "Let me stuff you in this stanza, before you overtake me again like a wave with a feline cry." (265) He fears the power of the woman within. She is the sea, the Amazon, the night, "the wave with the feline cry," the young girl at the window who was compared to a little tiger. The poet tries to get rid of her in order to do what he wants, for now, once again, he wants to play his accustomed roles before men without having her accuse him of inauthenticity or dissimulation. He wants to fulfill important duties recognized and approved by men like the builder of railroads or the union organizer. A young man with a blond beard who writes verse is not taken seriously; he is the object of derision.

The poet, now a mature man, believes that with the passage of time he should have been delivered of what he calls "the furies of this bacchic spirit" (266) whose laughter he hears in the innermost parts of his being. He asks that his muse at least allow him to write the way he wants. Like the Egyptian scribe and ancient sculptor, he wants his art to be his job. He would like to compose a great poem and forge a triumphant way in the land. Instead, he finds himself on the back of a winged horse that drags him along its broken course. Let us remember that in the Introduction he was the thoroughbred and his muse was the Amazon who rode him. Now he is the horseman and she is the horse, a winged steed. But he is still far from being able to subjugate her even though he now seems to have a semblance of control, since he is the rider.

He would like to celebrate everyday things in his verse, things that are recognizable and well-known. He would like, in some way, to keep accounts with his verse. But that idea makes her, the sister of the swarthy pythoness, indignant and she wounds him with her contemptuous gaze. The giantess rises with an air of sublime liberty. She is the wind on the desert, the beloved likened to Pharaoh's steeds. She becomes even more powerful when he resists her, when he tries to go his own way. He asserts that there is nothing in nature that was not made for man and it is the conquest of the earth that he wants to celebrate in verse and that he so admires, perhaps because he has not yet succeeded in conquering himself. What others have done with cannon, boats, batteries, with cities and ports, with locomotives and canals, he will do with a poem. It will be the great poem of the knowledge of the Earth and of man finally shielded from chance and reconciled with the eternal forces.

Yet one cannot help but ask if the poet himself has been reconciled with those eternal forces. That is what remains to be seen.

Antistanza I

The muse's voice is scornful. Of what importance are all those machines and the other things the poet values? She reproaches him for his attachment to the world, calling him a "big-footed clumsy clod born for the plow or to be a clerk." (268) She complains about her lot—an Immortal tied to a burdensome imbecile. Doesn't he know that it isn't with pen and ink that a living word is made, just as it isn't with a lathe and chisel that a living man is made. It's with a woman. And his muse is a woman among women. She is not accessible to reason and he will never dominate her. "You will not do with me what you want." (268) But she sings and dances and is beautiful. She demands fidelity and promises to share her immortality with him. He will always be young and handsome to her. Instead of reasoning, he should take advantage of this golden hour for she will not always be there. She is fragile on the earth's surface like someone bobbing up from beneath the water, or a bird who tries to alight, or the flame on the wick. She tries to teach him the great divine laugh. She wants him to look at her this brief moment for her face destroys death. He who drinks the new wine she offers is freed—he is no longer accountable to the creditor or the owner. All ties are loosened, even familial ties. She is a pagan goddess who wants to make him a god who could jump naked on stage with vines in his hair.

At this point one might ask if she wants to make him a god so that he might play another role, as the stage suggests, or so that he might transform reality into truth through art? Is the liberty she offers dangerous, linked as it is to pagan antiquity and that god on stage who brandishes a pigskin filled with wine?

Under the influence of her wine the drunkard sees double—things as they are and things as they are not—truth and the lie. And one suspects that the reality the poet wants to celebrate in verse is only a lie—the truth lies elsewhere. She also invites him to see the eternal morning, the earth and the sea under the morning sun like someone who appears before the throne of God or like the child Jupiter dazzled at the threshold of the cave in which he was born. She offers him the world for his inheritance as legitimate son, emphasizing the fact that the world was made for him and not he for the world.

Unfortunately, the freedom that she offers seems like a servitude to him and he resists. She tries to tell him that his attachment to the earth is the real servitude. She asks him to surrender and to overcome, to trample the earth, to tread it under foot like someone who is dancing. Joy is the irrefutable evidence that she is indeed proposing the right path to him. He, an immortal, was taking the perishable too seriously, instead of laughing at it. All he needs to transform the world is his gaze, the eyes of the spirit that sees and hears.

Stanza II

Resistance increases. What she proposes seems to him a temptation to be avoided. It would be like fleeing from life. She wants to drag him where he cannot fly and show him what he cannot see. She speaks of freedom but he has not yet fulfilled his obligations. She is a woman and as such she has no duty to fulfill. He cannot allow himself to be dominated by the woman within despite the sweetness of her laugh. It has been too hard becoming a man. (But is it really easier to surrender, to yield, than to triumph and to conquer?) He says that he has struggled to get used to those things which are not free, which one must take in order to possess. The passivity she seems to suggest terrifies him. His refusal will be definitive and even though his heart breaks, he says no. He rejects the light which he says is not for the sons of the earth.

The consequences of this refusal will be deadly. Darkness surrounds him and he is almost overcome. It is now that he prays for the first time in the poem; but despite this, he will have to suffer the consequences of his choice. The luminous young girl within, the little tiger, is transformed into a panther. Active shadows engulf him. The laughter deep within becomes the breath of Istar, goddess of the moon and of love. Now he feels the hand of the Mother of the Dead on his flesh.

To justify himself, he claims that it was his duty to resist. It was not his duty to leave, or to be any place else, or to give up what he has, or to win, but to resist and hold his ground. All his dreams of conquest disappear in the effort to justify himself. He rejects the sea saying that his cry is not the piercing cry of the Son of the Sea, but rather a human cry. He affirms that God has placed him on earth like a hewn stone that he might endure the discomfort, the constraint, the obscurity and the violence of the other stones that press against him. At all costs he wants to believe that his refusal was God's will and that what he has chosen was also His will. He prays that he will be protected against the beautiful temptress and her song. His bad faith disguises the real reasons for his refusal—fear of the opinion of others, fear of the freedom offered, fear of surrender and of losing control, the will to power, and his desire to conquer the world and gain the admiration of men. As Luce Irigaray informs us:

> The search for the perpetuation of one's identity stops all contact, paralyzes all penetration through fear of not finding oneself still and always the same. From this flows the metaphorizations [of men] in terms that envelop them, enfold them, separating them always more from what 'causes' them in associations that are nothing more than analogies[4]

—the analogy of the stone. The lie is subtle because he uses Biblical images to deceive. A hewn stone—what could be more worthy? We know that the church is

---

[4]Luce Irigaray, *Spéculum de l'autre femme* (Paris: Editions de minuit, 1974), 440. Translation mine. This source will be henceforth cited as *Sp*.

built of living stones and the master builder disposes of them as he desires. But a stone is hard and cannot be penetrated. It must be shattered if it does not conform to the wishes of the builder.

The truth finally penetrates his account and he cannot avoid saying: "Where can I follow her—after four steps she is no longer there?" (271) It is clear that he is fooling no one. The impulse to follow her remains because it is she that has a language which is finally real, a feminine sigh, an intelligible kiss, and the pure meaning ineffably contemplated of which he, with his art, creates a miserable shadow in letters and words. He knows perfectly well what he has just rejected. And it was useless to ask to be protected against her, as we shall see.

Antizanza II

His resistance has hardened him and has also hardened his interlocutor. He has chosen the Earth and its weight, but despite that, his muse will not abandon him. He did not want to learn joy from her, so he will have to learn pain, and also learn how to decipher her silent message and guess what she means. She will give him no rest. Clearly, he has misinterpreted everything up to this point, but she must communicate to him the rhythm she desires, even if it costs him his life. She will be demanding and cruel and she will make fun of him as she does when she says to him: "Stand up! walk in front of me, I want you to, / So that I can look at you and laugh, and so that I, the goddess, can imitate your mutilated gait!" (*Op* 272) Like the patriarch Jacob who struggled with the angel—like Turelure, hero of *The Hostage* and *Hard Bread*; like Rodrigue in *The Satin Slipper* and even Rimbaud ("La Messe Là-Bas," *Op* 512)—the poet cannot walk as other men. He emerges from his struggle against the woman within with wounded feet. He cannot fly because he is too heavy, but he cannot put his feet on the ground either. He will not find rest either in joy or in pain. He will not be that hewn stone placed on the earth to serve as foundation. She proposes to him another model: "A flame is also a foundation, / a dancing, halting flame, leaping and crackling with its uneven double tongue!" (*Op* 272)

Stanza III

Here the poet returns to her. His resistance has been useless; he knows that she will never abandon him. It is she who is his inspiration, that reserved part of himself, anterior to him—that idea of himself that existed before he did, his eternal likeness, the stranger who touches his heart certain nights. He and she are more unfortunate than those two astral lovers who see each other every year from opposite sides of the milky way without every being able to cross the chasm that separates them. We have here another appearance of the syzygy, the conjunction and opposition of the masculine and feminine principles.

Now he asks her to look at him, ridiculous, wounded, and stifled as he is among men. The stone can no longer endure its vocation as stone. Now he desires a word, a word which is at once human and divine—his name, his real name, his new name, "in the fullness of the Earth, in the nuptials of the night's sun," (*Op* 273) not one of those terrible, silent words that she occasionally communicates to him that are like a cross to which his spirit remains nailed. And all of that means that he desires the new life but without renouncing the old one—to be reborn without dying—celestial nuptials without the cross. "O the passion of the Word!" he exclaims, "withdrawal! terrible solitude! separation from all men! my own death and the death of all things, in which I must undergo creation!" (*Op* 273) We encounter a fear even more fundamental than the fear of being dominated—a fear of loneliness, separation, and death. And he has been struggling against these enemies for a long time. We learn that even when he was a little boy, this sister, this guide, this merciless one was there. Will he always be an odd and unique man, full of worries and works, subject to a woman over whom he has no power, who goes and comes as she wants? He, as all men, dreams of acquiring a woman at the right age and being with her like a closed circle and like a impregnable city, like the faultless union of the beginning and the end. And here we perceive once again his enduring desire to be a stone—round, impenetrable, hewn but still intact. This dream is in the image of the masculine idea of God:

> That God could have been conceived as a perfect volume, a closed
> fullness, an infinite circle in the amplitude of all extension, is certainly
> not a product of the imagination [of woman]. This passion for an origin
> duly encircled even at the risk of biting once again the end of one's own

tail, for a dwelling shut tight so that "it" eventually happens, for a womb closed on the inside, is certainly not hers. (*Sp* 293)

Woman

> remains the exterior of the circularity of a thought that in its telos reappropriates for itself the cause of its desire: the unconscious support of the attempt to metaphorize a matrix in the sphere of personal intimacy, of nearness to self, of a 'soul,' or a spirit. She remains everything in the site that cannot be gathered in a place.... (*Sp* 297-98)

Who then can know what she is asking for? She murmurs in his ear and he thinks he hears that it is the whole world she desires. She wants him, but because he is not whole without the world that surrounds him, he is sure that it is the whole world that she demands. When he hears her call, every being is necessary for unanimity. But is he certain he has understood what she requires? One has doubts when he exclaims: "To whom am I necessary, if not to you who do not say want you want." (*Op* 274) Can he be mistaken once again, blinded as he is by his fear of loneliness, separation, and death? Will he once again try to trick her. He claims that when she calls him it is not by himself that he must respond, but with all the beings that surround him. (See *Sp* 440 above.) He is being asked, he believes, for a whole poem which would be like one word, an enclosed city, or the circle of the mouth. It is the whole world that he must offer, like a great sacrifice, with a hecatomb of words. Despite the fact that he does not see her, he knows that it is in her that he finds his necessity and that all things are necessary to him through her. It is not for him that they were made, their order is not with him but with her—the word that created them.

He finally decides to give himself because she demands it, but for him to do so he says he must find himself in all things because he is the Host, the latent sign, in all things. But why does one still hear the same question? "What do you want of me? is it necessary to create the world to understand it? Is it necessary for me to engender the world and give birth to it? My own creation brought forth in pain! Oh the effort of the world to represent you!"? (*Op* 274) Must he allow himself to be transformed, to be feminized, in order to assume a maternal creative function? One must answer both yes and no at the same time. Having rejected the sea,

> it is then at once the amniotic fluid, the most profound sea, that escapes
> him as well as what represents feminine pleasure…a movement of the
> sea, back and forth, a continual flux…completely foreign to what is an
> economy of erection and detumescence… scaling the mountain and
> descending the mountain[5]

And one hears the poet say:

> And like a huge mountain that divides its simultaneous waters between
> contrary water basins,
> So it is that I work and will never know what I have done, so the spirit
> with a mortal spasm
> Ejects the word outside of him like a spring of water that knows
> nothing other than its pressure and the weight of the heavens. (275)

He divides these simultaneous waters between contrary water basins like he divided himself in this ode—he and his muse, really identical, split between opposing sides, one masculine and the other feminine. As he says elsewhere: "One must divide in order to understand. And oneself, why not…introduce dialogue and controversy between the left and the right of one's spirit.[6] But this woman within also participates in a reality outside of him, which he has perhaps eschewed in rejecting the sea.

Antistanza III

That woman is also Grace—the word of grace addressed to him alone. She loves him and chose him before he was born. She has sought him out to tell him not to try to deceive her, to give her the world in his place. It is he that she wants. The moment has come when he, the uniter of images and of cities and of all men, must unite himself. She exhorts him to "Be a single spirit! be of one intention!" (*Op* 275) She also informs him that it is fire pure and simple that makes of many things only one and

---

[5]Luce Irigaray, *Le corps-à-corps avec la mère* (Montréal: Les éditions de la pleine lune, 1981), 48-49. Translation mine.

[6]Paul Claudel, *Emmaüs, Oeuvres complètes*, Vol. 25 (Paris: Gallimard, 1964), 300. Translation mine. Henceforth cited as *Oc*.

it is death that calls all things into life. He was born for that death in her. As the sun calls everything into birth (*naissance*), the spirit calls all things to rebirth (*connaissance* —knowledge). And after the abundance of April and superabundance of summer, there is the work of August, the extermination of noon when God's seals are broken and the earth is judged by fire, when heaven and earth become a single nest in the flames of their destruction. Noon is the time when there are no shadows. Irigaray explains that "man, at first, eludes the confrontation with his shadow. Black expanse lying at his feet on the ground. Headed west, it is, as it were, hidden from him. Still behind. It is under the covering of others' shadows—the shadows of other men or things—that he advances towards the sun." (*Sp* 358-59) At noon in August, one has no shadow; but if, at that moment, one does not decide to turn towards the light, from then on, one will have that shadow ahead and the light behind.

Epode

Here is his response to the call of Grace: "Go away!" (276) He turns desperately toward the earth whose cold taste is rooted in his hard substance—his stony substance, the black kernel of his viscera. The more she calls him, the more he withdraws towards the ground like a great tree. She will not consume him with her fiery presence. He has bitten the earth, like Adam the apple, and the taste is still in his mouth. He has tasted blood and he no longer wants glimmering water or burning honey. He has loved a human soul and been united to it. Something in him now lives off the bread of another body. He has been captured forever.

What has he chosen then? —his ancient sister of darkness in the profound night, his nocturnal spouse, who comes to him once again with his heart like a repast to be shared, like the bread of pain and a vase full of tears. In the last image, the water of the beginning is completely devoid of light. It is the entrance to Hell that the poet has before him, "that low canal that is not even lit by the ray of a leaden star and the lugubrious horn of Hecate." (*Op* 277)

Although some commentators have attributed the tragic dualism in Claudel's feminine images to his personal history with eroticism, it cannot be denied that the interior struggle depicted in this ode characterizes all of Claudel's work. In my book

Women and the Feminine Principle in the Works of Paul Claudel, [7] I explain it in two ways. There is, of course, the erotic challenge tied to the experience of adultery and feminine betrayal in his personal story. But there is another desire, as fundamental as erotic desire, and a fear which is even more fundamental—the desire to conquer and dominate, the will to power, on the one hand; and the fear of death, on the other, "the fear of not finding oneself to be still and always the same." (*Sp* 440) Those are Claudel's real motives. He is then dishonest even in the Epode. It is not simply because he has loved another soul that he will not surrender, but also because he fears allowing himself to be penetrated by Grace. He fears losing control of himself. He fears death.

The most disturbing attribute of Claudel's muse was undoubtedly her independence. It would seem that man will never succeed in dominating his dreams, his inspiration or his soul. Also disturbing was the fact that his muse, the woman within, would lead him where he feared to go. She would have him abandon reason and duty, or so it seemed. We heard the poet resist, crying out: "It has been so hard becoming a man," (*Op* 270) a remark which betrays the intensity of his inner struggle. There is in the poet a tension, for Claudel a violent tension, between inspiration and rational mastery which is associated with becoming a man.

We have also once again encountered the intuition that this female presence somehow represents the divine. The Father's voice is clearly mediated though this feminine presence which the poet resists in his quest for rational self-sufficiency and mastery. Yet we saw that resistance to her, despite the threats she represents, only led to sterility and death. There is danger on all sides—the danger of the uncontrollable which she represents and the danger of the illusion of self-sufficiency and mastery which she disrupts. Both have their allure.

Claudel often reminds us that most of his work represents an effort to shed light on his interior drama and that most of the characters in his plays represent different

---

[7]See Ann Bugliani, *Women and the Feminine Principle in the Works of Paul Claudel*, (Madrid: Porrúa-Turranzas, 1977). Henceforth cited as B.

aspects of himself. For him, one of the prime purposes of art is, indeed, the purge of the soul. He speaks of deliverance through creation and of the violent struggle which filled the first twenty years of his literary life—the struggle for complete mastery over himself. Claudel's characters were as independent as was his muse. They followed their own logic and often developed and acted in ways which surprised and even disturbed the poet. (B 105-06) The poet is, in fact, at the mercy of inspiration, as Plato affirmed. But because the poet does not completely banish these dangerous elements, as does the philosopher, there will emerge from his creativity certain truths—a certain wisdom—to which all should give heed.

CHAPTER 3

WHAT TRAGEDY TEACHES

Let us now turn our focus from poetry to tragedy and attempt to understand its nature and what it teaches us, especially in the ethical domain, by examining some contemporary theories of tragedy. We will then consider some current views concerning what literature in general teaches us, particularly in regard to ethics, but also in regard to desire. Before doing any of this, however, we must revisit Plato, for it is important to note that his attitude, which was discussed in Chapter 1, is in marked contrast to Aristotle's. Aristotle has a high regard for tragedy. In his discussion of the education of young citizens, he gives it a place of honor. The value he attributes to emotions and feelings naturally leads him to reconsider the texts that Plato had banished.

Martha Nussbaum[1] explains that Aristotle believes that emotions are individuated not simply by the way they feel but, more importantly, by the kinds of judgments or beliefs that are internal to each. A typical Aristotelian emotion is defined as a composite of a feeling of either pleasure or pain and a particular type of belief about the world. Anger, for example, is a composite of painful feeling with the belief that one has been wronged. The feeling and the belief are not just incidentally linked: the belief is the ground of the feeling. If it were found by the agent to be false, the feeling would not persist; or, if it did, it would no longer persist as a constituent in that emotion. It is

---

[1]Martha C. Nussbaum, *The Fragility of Goodness. Luck and Ethics in Greek Tragedy and Philosophy* (Cambridge: Cambridge University Press, 1986), 383. Henceforth cited as *F*.

part of the same view that emotions may be assessed as either rational or irrational, 'true' or 'false', depending upon the nature of their grounding beliefs. If my anger is based upon a hastily adopted false belief concerning a wrong done me, it may be criticized as both irrational and 'false.' (*F* 383)

For Aristotle, pity has great value as a human response. Through pity we recognize and acknowledge the importance of what has been inflicted on another human being similar to us, through no fault of their own. As we pay attention to our responses of pity, we can hope to learn more about our own implicit view of what is important in human life, about the vulnerability of our own deepest commitments.

Fear is intimately connected with pity. Aristotle stresses repeatedly that what we pity another for, we fear for ourselves. And since pity already requires the perception of one's own vulnerability, one's similarity to the sufferer, then pity and fear will almost always occur together. Fear is defined as a pain or disturbance due to a mental picture of some destructive or painful evil in the future.[2] If, as Aristotle urges, we acknowledge the tragic characters as similar to us, we will, with and in our fear, acknowledge their tragedy as a possibility for ourselves. And such a response will itself be an insight into our human situation and our values.

We can connect his demand for similarity between ourselves and the hero with his ranking of poetry above history as a source of wisdom. History, he points out, tells us what in fact happened; poetry, what might have happened. History tells us the particular, such as what so and so did or suffered; poetry, the general or universal, the sort of thing that happens to certain sorts of people. Poetry is then something more philosophic and of graver import than history, since its statements are of the nature of universals, whereas those of history are singulars.[3] Nussbaum adds the suggestion that events narrated by history are so idiosyncratic that they prevent identification. (*F* 386)

She judiciously concludes that for Aristotle the viewing of pitiable and

---

[2] Aristotle, *Rhetoric, The Works of Aristotle* (Chicago: William Benton, 1952), 1382a21.

[3] Aristotle, *Poetics,* 1451b4-11.

fearful things in tragedy, *and* our responses of pity and fear themselves, can serve to show us something of importance about the human good. For the Platonist or the good-condition theorist, they cannot. For Aristotle, pity and fear will be sources of illumination or clarification (catharsis), as the agent, responding and attending to his or her responses, develops a richer self-understanding concerning the attachments and values that support the responses. For Aristotle's opponents, pity and fear can never be better than sources of delusion and obfuscation. (*F* 388)

Aristotle's philosophical opponents insist that if a person's character is good, the person cannot be harmed in any serious way. In their view, there is no room, conceptually, for pity. Plato indeed repudiates pity in the strongest terms. Plato's argument is that correct beliefs about what is and is not important in human life remove our reasons for fear. (*F* 385-86) Nussbaum contends that to a middle period Platonist, it would be profoundly shocking to read of cognitive clarification produced by the influence of pity and fear: first, because the Platonic soul attains clarity only when no emotions disturb it; second, because these emotions are especially irrational. But we know that in Aristotle's view, tragedy contributes to human self-understanding, to clarification, precisely through its exploration of the pitiable and the fearful. The exploration is carried out by moving us to respond with these very emotions. Just as in *Antigone*, Creon learned through the grief he felt for his son's death, so, as we watch a tragic character, it is frequently not thought but the emotional response itself that leads us to understand what our values are. Emotions can sometimes mislead and distort judgment; Aristotle is aware of this. But they can also—as was true in Creon's case—give us access to a truer and deeper level of ourselves, to values and commitments that have been concealed beneath defensive ambition or rationalization. (*F* 390)

We know that the Anglo-American philosophical tradition has tended to assume that the ethical text should, in the process of inquiry, converse with the intellect alone: it should not make its appeal to the emotions, feelings, and sensory responses. This mind-set in the Anglo-American tradition goes back at least as far as Locke, who writes, in terms reminiscent of Plato, that the rhetorical and emotive elements of style are rather like a woman: amusing and even delightful when kept in their place, dangerous and corrupting if permitted to take control. We know, too, that Kant considered desire to be intrinsically hostile to rationality. Yet it is clear that a work of tragic poetry must also engage our emotions. Our cognitive activity, as we explore the ethical conception embodied in the text, centrally involves emotional response. We discover what we think about the events portrayed partly by noticing how we feel; our investigation of our emotions is a major part of our search for self-knowledge. Nussbaum will argue that emotional response can sometimes be not just a *means* to practical knowledge, but a constituent part of the best sort of recognition or knowledge of one's practical situation. (*F* 15-16)

There is a two-way interchange of illumination and cultivation working between emotions and thoughts: feelings are prepared by memory and deliberation, learning is brought about through *pathos*. When we notice the ethical fruitfulness of these exchanges, when we see the *rationality* of the passions as they lead thought towards human understanding, and help to constitute this understanding, then we may feel that the burden of proof is shifted to the defender of the view that only intellect and will are appropriate objects of ethical assessment. Such a conception may begin to look impoverished. The plays show us the practical wisdom and ethical accountability of a contingent mortal being in a world of natural happening. Such a being is neither a pure intellect nor a pure will; nor would he deliberate better in this world if he were. (*F* 47)

As I have already noted, for the Greeks content is not separable from poetic style. To become a poet was not regarded by them as an ethically neutral matter. As we have seen, stylistic choices—the selection of certain meters, certain patterns of image and vocabulary—are taken to be closely bound up with a conception of the good. The dialogue, for instance, can show us moral development and change taking place. The dramatic poem can show us the forces that lead to change or increased self-knowledge, and the fruits of change in practical life. This is a part of learning that non-dramatic didactic moral texts deny us. (*F* 128)

The claim is also made in the Anglo-American tradition that the human being's relation to the world is not, or should not be, profoundly tragic: that it is, or should be, possible without serious loss to cut off the risk of the typical tragic occurrence. Tragedy would then represent a primitive or benighted stage of ethical life and thought. (*F* 51) It would, along with the theological, mark the infancy of the race or the first stage of man's intellectual experience. Both would be banished by the metaphysical, marking the second stage. The final stage, ours, has also repudiated the metaphysical in favor of the scientific.[4]

In commenting on this perspective, Murray Krieger speaks scathingly of the "unearned optimism" and the self-deceptions of those who, for all the hardheadedness of their religious disbelief, are still naive believers in social progress. These are, he says, the men of little heart who, evading the atheist's existential obligation to confront nothingness and its frightening empty consequences, construct elaborate rational structures based on nothing else: who whistle in the dark as if all were light. Krieger feels that their cheerfully naturalistic vision is pampering in its security because it denies itself nothing despite the fearsome implications of its own metaphysical denials. It existentially shirks the void it must rationally insist upon. The naturalist, Krieger notes, tries to play both sides of the street to earn the prize of an ungrounded something: "a world philosophically negated which is somehow made to yield the existential ease that would come if there were meaning and purpose to be grasped."[5]

Nietzsche, of course, points to another way out. John Sallis notes that for him art is not merely imitation of the reality of nature, but rather a metaphysical

---

[4]Michael Lacey, *Conversations* 8 (1995): 9. Max Scheler (*Le phénomène du tragique* [Paris: Aubier, 1952], 112-13) explains that the tragic can indeed not exist in a universe in which values have no place, a universe such as the one constructed by purely mechanical physics. Only where there is the superior and the inferior, the noble and the vulgar, can something similar to tragic events exist. Values are of course not tragic in and of themselves but the tragic only manifests itself in things, men, and events through the intermediary of the values that are attached to them. The tragic is then always sustained or founded by values and the relationships among values. For tragedy to manifest itself, a value must be destroyed. Man need not be annihilated, but something in him—a project, an intention, a force, a good, a belief—must be destroyed. It is not, however, this destruction that is tragic, but the fact that positive values—values which are inferior or equivalent, but never superior to the endangered value—direct their action toward this destruction.

[5]Murray Krieger, *The Tragic Vision* (New York: Holt, Rinehart, and Winston, 1960), 14-16.

supplement of it, placed beside it for its overcoming.[6] Tragedy discloses nature, or rather that divergence from nature within nature that constitutes the abyss. Pessimism is, understandably, the threat brought on by exposure to the Dionysian abyss and it is this precisely that is overcome by tragedy. Nietzsche says that tragedy is the natural healing power against the Dionysian.[7] Tragedy alone knows how to turn dreadful thoughts about the horror of existence into representations with which we can live. Tragedy exposes us to the abyss, and yet, in this very disclosure protects, saves, even heals us from the destructive consequences that such exposure can have. Tragedy leads us back, leaves us finally comforted, by letting the horrible turn into the sublime.[8] It might be said that the sublime is then the artistic taming of the horrible. Exposing us mimetically to the abyss, tragedy at the same time lets the abyss be displaced, lets it be replaced with the sublime. (*N* 93) Nietzsche speaks of the truly serious task of art which he describes as saving the eye from gazing into the horrors of night and delivering the subject by the healing balm of shining.[9] For Nietzsche tragedy is no mere temporary masking of the source of human misery, but rather a disclosure capable of leading us back from pessimism to affirmation. The disclosure in question is precisely that of the abyss as sublime.

In discussing the tension between tragic drama and the theoretical attitude with its demand for final transparency, Sallis warns that in tragedy there are points beyond which the phenomenon itself precludes transparency and resists accounting. A

---

[6] John Sallis, *Crossings: Nietzsche and the Space of Tragedy* (Chicago: University of Chicago Press, 1991), 83. Henceforth cited as *N*.

[7] *Notebooks* III 3:69 cited in *N* 92.

[8] Jean-François Lyotard in "The Sublime and the Avant-Garde" (*Artforum*, [April 1984]: 40) has this to say concerning the sublime sensation: "A very big, very powerful object threatens to deprive the soul of any and all 'happenings,' stuns it (at lower intensities, the soul is at this point seized with admiration, veneration, respect). The soul is dumb, immobilized, as good as dead. Art, by distancing this menace, procures a pleasure of relief, of delight. Thanks to art, the soul is returned to the agitated zone between life and death, and this agitation is its health and its life."

[9] *Notebooks* III 1:122 cited in *N* 97-98.

theoretical account of tragedy will encounter limits. There is then a sense in which we must simply submit ourselves to tragedy. Since the demand for final transparency is coupled with a desire for mastery, this submission itself is feared and resisted, as we have seen.

In this context, we can appreciate the novelty of Nussbaum's method and the obvious difference between the way in which some recent philosophers, for example Sidgwick and Rawls, have pursued an Aristotelian ethical inquiry and her procedure in *The Fragility of Goodness*. This is that she has chosen to consult certain texts, namely four tragic dramas, that are traditionally considered to be works of 'literature' rather than works of 'philosophy'. In the Anglo-American tradition it is customary to consider literary and philosophical texts to be different, bearing in different ways on human ethical questions. Yet, she insists, this was clearly not the view of the Greeks. For them there were human lives and problems, and various genres in both prose and poetry in which one could reflect about those problems. As we have seen, epic and tragic poets were widely assumed to be the central ethical thinkers and teachers of Greece; nobody thought of their work as less serious, less aimed at truth, than the prose treatises of historians and philosophers. *(F* 12)[10]

---

[10]Edwin Rohde corroborates this in *Psyche* (New York: Harper & Row, 1966). He informs us that "it was not until the rise in later times of a fully developed philosophy extending its range of interpretation to the whole of life that poetry was deprived of its special office of instructress to the aspiring minds among people. Poetry had always been willing to exercise this function, but never so decidedly or with such fully conscious purpose as in the times of transition at the beginning of which Pindar lived—the transition from an unsophisticated faith in the traditional view of all things visible and invisible to a fresh stabilization of belief secured by, and resting upon, philosophic conviction. The need felt for the readjustment or verification of the ancestral or traditional forms of belief was vividly awakened, and it was still only poetry that could extend the light of its teaching to illuminate the minds of whole classes of the population. The influence of the poets must have increased in proportion as the numbers increased of those who were ready to receive the special bounty which they were able to offer. But if the influence wielded by Pindar, the Pan-Hellenic poet of the great Festivals, as the teacher of his people was . . . considerable, a very wide field indeed for the propagation of fruitful ideas lay open to the Attic tragedians in the huge concourse of the people which flocked together to hear their creations—a multitude which seemed all the greater for being confined within a narrower space. The poets themselves frequently allow it to be seen how seriously they regarded themselves as the teachers of their public, and the people admitted their claims. All men expected and demanded instruction from the word of the poet—the highest instruction from the highest poetry." (420-21)

Nussbaum's intent, then, was to study the works of the tragic poets as ethical reflection in their own right, embodying in both their content and their style a conception of human excellence. She regards them as creations of the 'wise,' as works of distinction to which a culture looked for insight. They are unlikely to conceal from view the vulnerability of human lives to fortune, the mutability of our circumstances and our passions, and the existence of conflicts among our commitments. A philosophical work of the type most familiar in the Anglo-American tradition, one that does not focus intently on the stories of concrete characters, can lose all of these facts from view in the pursuit of systematic considerations or to the end of greater purity. (*F* 13) Nussbaum's whole enterprise in *The Fragility of Goodness* involves a challenge to those who affirm the self-sufficiency of reason and who are overly optimistic about their grasp and control of practical problems. (*F* 125)

In the same vein, Gellrich remarks that critical theory, especially Hegel's ethical brand, is rather like the law in that it formulates strategies to subdue the complexities and recalcitrant moral ambivalences dramatized in the struggles of tragedy. (*C* 68) By imposing an orderly teleology on the collisions and contradictions of the play, one can guarantee mediation that secures the ultimate unity sought by critics of tragedy from the time of Aristotle. But the insistence on unity leads away from an appreciation of the strategies in tragedy that disrupt our categories of understanding and expose the inconsistencies of moral standards. (*C* 71)

To summarize, then, I would say that the impulse to banish tragedy which persists, now primarily in the Anglo-American tradition, is indeed an impulse driven by the fear—fear of death, as Derrida claims—for it would veil a certain truth concerning the vulnerability of human life, its mutability, its susceptibility to conflict and its moral ambivalences and inconsistencies. It would, in Sallis' terms, close off the abyss, leaving it sealed and forgotten like an abandoned mine or cave. (*N* 91)

Another contemporary thinker who unequivocally affirms the teaching of tragedy is Paul Ricoeur, notably in *Oneself As Another*.[11] He notes that the instruction of tragedy is not a direct, univocal, or moral teaching; it instead carries practical wisdom back to the test of judgment in situation. He agrees that *Antigone*, for instance, says something unique about the unavoidable nature of conflict in moral life. It outlines a wisdom capable of directing us in conflicts by showing us conflicts that are intractable and not open to negotiation. Tragedy is comparable to aporia—producing limit experiences. *Antigone* posited the limit that points up the human character of every institution.The instruction of ethics by tragedy comes out of the recognition of this limit. What is sketched out is not a teaching, but a manner of looking which ethics will work to extend in its own discourse. Catharsis, of course, addresses itself directly to the passions, not only provoking them but purifying them as well. Ricoeur claims that the metaphorization of terror and pity is the very condition for all properly ethical instruction. The purgative effect of the spectacle itself is at the center of the passions it produces. Tragic catharsis, although giving no direct counsel, opens the path to the moment of conviction through a meditation on the inevitable place of conflict in moral life. There is an appeal to think correctly. Tragedy creates a gap between tragic wisdom and practical wisdom refusing to contribute a solution to conflicts made insoluble by fiction. One is forced to reorient action, at one's own risk, in the sense of practical wisdom in situation that best responds to tragic wisdom. Conviction becomes the haven beyond catharsis. He notes correctly in *The Symbolism of Evil*[12] that ethical denunciation and reform is not the business of tragedy as it was to be in comedy. The tragic hero is shielded from moral condemnation and offered as an object of pity to the chorus and the spectator.[13]

---

[11]Paul Ricoeur, *Oneself As Another*, trans. Kathleen Blamey (Chicago: University of Chicago Press, 1992), 241-47. Henceforth cited as *One*.

[12]Paul Ricoeur, *The Symbolism of Evil*, trans. Emerson Buchanan (New York: Harper and Row, 1967), 219. Henceforth cited as *S*.

[13]Ricoeur also observes that without the dialectics of fate and freedom there would be no tragedy. Tragedy requires, on the one hand, transcendence, and, more precisely, hostile transcendence; and on the other, the upsurge of freedom that delays the fulfillment of fate, causes it to hesitate and to appear contingent at the height of the crisis, in order finally to make it break out in a "dénouement," where its fatal character is ultimately revealed. Without the delaying action of the freedom of the

Finally, we should add that salvation, in the tragic vision, is not outside the tragic but within it. This is the meaning of that suffering which is celebrated by the chorus in Aeschylus' *Agamemnon*:   "In suffering he lays foundations deep of knowledge."[14]

---

hero, fate would be comparable to a discharge of lightening, the freedom of the hero introduces into the heart of the inevitable a germ of uncertainty, a termporary delay, thanks to which there is a "drama "—that is to say, an action the outcome of which, while it is taking place, is uncertain. Thus delayed by the hero, fate, implacable in itself, deploys itself in a venture that seems contingent to us; thus is born the tragic action with its peculiar cruelty. The unstable mixture of certainty and surprise is turned to terror by the drop of transcendent perfidy that tragic theology lets fall on it. (*S* 220-21)

"Man's share" must at least begin to be discerned if the ethical moment in evil is to appear; there must be at least an indication of a dawn of responsibility, of avoidable fault, and guilt must begin to be distinguished from finiteness. But this distinction tends to be muted, annulled by predestination; the indistinctness of divine and human guilt is an incipient and annulled distinction. (*S* 222)

[14]Aeschylus, *Agamemnon, The Plays of Aeschylus*, trans. G. M. Cookson (Chicago: William Benton, 1952), 177-79.

Literature, Ethics, and Psychoanalysis

Turning our attention now to literature in general, it is interesting to note that Goethe was dubious about the ability of literature to affect the moral education of the mind. He felt that it was wrong to expect it to do so. Only philosophy and religion could achieve this.[15] Ricoeur, in contrast, asserts that in literature we experiment with estimations, evaluations, and judgments of approval and condemnation through which narrativity serves as a propaedeutic to ethics. (*One* 115) It is in literary fiction that the connection between action and its agent is easiest to perceive and literature proves to be an immense laboratory for thought experiments in which this connection is submitted to an endless number of imaginative variations.

But how do the thought experiments occasioned by fiction, with all their ethical implications, contribute to self-examination in real life? Ricoeur observes that the possibility of applying literature to life rests upon the problem of identification-with. (*One* 159) He also points to Benjamin's characterization of the art of story-telling as the art of exchanging experiences or the popular exercise of practical wisdom. This wisdom always includes estimations, evaluations that fall under teleological and deontological categories. In the exchange of experiences which the narrative performs, actions are always subject to approval or disapproval and agents to praise or blame.

In fact, in the unreal sphere of fiction we never tire of exploring new ways of evaluating actions and characters. The thought experiments we conduct in the great laboratory of the imaginary are also explorations in the realm of good and evil. Transvaluing, even devaluing, is still evaluating. Moral judgment has not been abolished; but is itself subjected to the imaginative variations proper to fiction.

Ricoeur also argues that if the aim of the true life, which MacIntyre, echoing Aristotle, places at the summit of the hierarchy of the levels of praxis, is to become a

---

[15]Johann Wolfgang von Goethe, *Essays on Art and Literature*, ed. John Geary, trans. Ellen von Nardroff and Ernest H. von Nardroff (New York: Suhrkamp Publishers, 1983), 199.

vision, it cannot help but be depicted in the narratives through which we try out different courses of action by playing with competing possibilities. This allows us to speak of an "ethical imagination" which feeds off the narrative imagination. (*One* 164-65)

In *Freud and Philosophy*,[16] Ricoeur maintains that the production of dreams and the creation of works of art represent two ends of the scale according to whether the predominant emphasis in the symbolism is disguise or disclosure, distortion or revelation. By this formula he attempts to account both for the functional unity existing between dreams and creativity and for the difference in value that separates a mere product of our dreams from the lasting works that become a part of the cultural heritage of mankind. Between dreams and artistic creativity there is a functional continuity, in the sense that disguise and disclosure are operative in both of them, but in an inverse proportion.[17] That is why, he says, Freud is justified in moving from one to the other by a series of imperceptible transitions, as he does in "Creative Writers and Daydreaming." Passing from night dreams to daydreams, from daydreams to play and humor, then to folklore and legends, and finally to works of art, he attests, by this species of increasingly closer analogy, that all creativity is involved in the same economic function and brings about the same substitution of satisfaction as the compromise formations of dreams and the neuroses.

If Oedipus Rex or Hamlet are creations, they are so in the measure that they are not mere projections of the artist's conflicts, but also the sketch of their solution. Because of the emphasis on disguise, dreams look more to the past, to childhood. But in works of art the emphasis is on disclosure; thus works of art tend to be prospective symbols of one's personal synthesis and of man's future and not merely a regressive symptom of the artist's unresolved conflicts.

Ricoeur sums up the role of all art when he states that the exploration of

---

[16]Paul Ricoeur, *Freud and Philosophy: An Essay on Interpretation*, trans. Denis Savage (New Haven: Yale University Press, 1970), 520-21. Henceforth Cited as *Fr*.

[17] See Chapter 6 on Dramatic Creation.

human possibilities extends into the objectivity of works or cultural objects. Painted, sculptured, or written works give these "images of man" the density of thingness, the stability of reality, they make these images exist between people and among people by embodying them in the material of stone, color, musical score, or the written word. It is through the medium of these works or monuments that a certain dignity of man is formed, which is the instrument and trace of a process of replicated consciousness, of recognition of the self in another self. (*Fr* 523)

René Girard, has also explored the instruction contained in literature. He states in *Critiques dans un souterrain*[18] that he does not believe that he is succumbing to a mysticism concerning the work of art or a religious mysticism when we says that he believes that there exists in certain literary works a knowledge concerning desire which is superior to anything that has ever been proposed by psychology or psychoanalysis. He is not impugning science; he is merely concerned with seeking knowledge wherever it may be found, regardless of how unexpected that place may be.

He obviously clashes with the tradition that associates all serious scientific research with a certain type of didactic exposition, that is, with the abandonment of all fiction and drama. The meaning of an interpretation is given *a priori*. Everything must emanate from explicitly scientific works and return to them. The idea, for instance, that Dostoevski could have something to teach Freud, that he could be more capable of interpreting Freud than Freud of interpreting himself doesn't occur to Freud. The striking intuitions of an author are not ignored by him, but it is assumed that these intuitions will be fragmentary, that they will never form a coherent whole. The dominance of psychoanalysis goes unchallenged. Freud acknowledges that Dostoevski has certain timely intuitions of truth, but it is a truth which will be essentially found in Freud. It is the scientist or theoretician who will always figure as supreme arbiter and absolute frame of reference.

Girard claims that Freud treats literature as a sort of magic charm. For him the

---

[18]René Girard, *Critique dans un souterrain* (Paris: Grasset, 1976), 36. Henceforth cited as *Cs*.

works of Dostoevski, and even literature considered as a whole, are a homogeneous mass, a seamless block of repression and sublimation. Freud never accepts the idea that the work of a writer could be the fruit of an intellectual enterprise like his own, with its inevitable errors, its botched experiments, its risks of definitive failure but also its chances of success, everything that is implied in the admirable expression *by trial and error*. He never concedes to the writer the exercise of real thought or the intellectual adventure in its fullest sense.

Girard feels that if the scientific pretensions which have dominated three quarters of the twentieth century are in the end shown to be disappointing and deceptive, one must first of all admit it to oneself, without falling into the defeatism which denies all science or doesn't believe it to be possible until man is eliminated. We must retrieve what failing dogmatisms have disdained, the great literary masterpieces. We are not to pass from one idolatry to another and to canonize all literary types indiscriminately. We should instead lend an ear, in a climate cleansed of scientific terrorism and aesthetic futility, to those authors who could go further than any have ever been in the knowledge of the relationships of desire. (*Cs* 39-40) Emanuel Berman makes a similar point in his introduction to *Essential Papers on Literature and Psychoanalysis* when he remarks that analysts are intrigued by literature and are attracted to it, but take it for granted that they have an exclusive capacity to master it. He exhorts therapists and diagnosticians to abandon their pretentious attitude toward "disturbed" literary figures or authors and adopt a greater willingness to let "literature be our therapist, that is, to allow it to teach us new ways of looking at ourselves."[19]

Jacques Lacan certainly gives heed to the instruction of literature. He points to catharsis, which he says involves the purification of desire, as a factor that unites psychoanalysis and tragedy. He, too, reminds us that Aristotle teaches that this purification cannot occur until we pass through terror and pity. Like Nussbaum, Lacan says that our reaction to the spectacle will indeed teach us something about

---

[19]Emanuel Berman, "Introduction," *Essential Papers on Literature and Psychoanalysis*, ed. Emanuel Berman (New York: New York University Press, 1993), 3-4.

what is hidden deep within us. Like Ricoeur he affirms that the teaching of tragedy is not a moral teaching, in the ordinary sense of the word, although he speaks of the ethical nature of catharsis. He tells us in his *Ethics*[20] that he was forced to turn to tragedy, as Freud was, to make himself understood. The ethics of psychoanalysis is not a speculation on the order or arrangement of what might be called the service of the various goods. It implies, to be accurate, the dimension which is expressed in the tragic experience of life. It is in this tragic dimension that actions are inscribed and that we are encouraged to take our bearings in our search for values. We shall see that in his seminars to analysts in training he turns to tragic literature, not merely to make himself understood, however; but also to understand man's desire.

We note then that at a time when many concede the failure of the enlightenment project with its deification of reason and its often thoughtless optimism, some of the foremost contemporary figures in psychoanalysis and philosophy, look to literature, notably the tragedies of Paul Claudel, for wisdom, tragic wisdom, if you will, concerning the human condition.

---

[20]Jacques Lacan, *L'éthique de la psychanalyse* (Paris: Editions du Seuil, 1986), 361. Henceforth cited as *E*.

CHAPTER 4

JACQUES LACAN READS PAUL CLAUDEL

In Jacques Lacan's Seminar on the transference stage in psychotherapy[1] which took place in 1960-1961 but was published in 1991, he states that man's desire has been the pervading focus of all his teaching. He describes his method as one of alternating between scientific definition, in its broadest sense, and the analysis of something quite different—that of the experience found in tragedy. In 1958 his focus was *Hamlet*. The following year he examined the significance of ancient tragedy by studying *Antigone*. Here, in *Le Transfert*, he speaks of exploring contemporary experience in search of an exemplar of human desire which would serve to illustrate his thought. Freud's insights could not possibly have emerged by happenstance, in isolation. Surely modern times, which have seen the birth of psychoanalytic thought, provide all the elements necessary for drama, the drama which emerges when it is a question of desire and its obstacles. (*T* 316)

Lacan finds his exemplar of modern tragedy in Paul Claudel's Coûfontaine trilogy—*L'Otage* (*The Hostage*), *Le Pain dur* (*Hard Bread*), and *Le Père humilié* (*The Humiliated Father*). He calls it a contemporary rendering of the myth of Oedipus and delights in telling us the story of his find.

He had not reread the Trilogy for a long time. He was instead reading the Gide/Claudel correspondence which he recommended to his students, despite some

---

[1]*Le Séminaire de Jacques Lacan*, Livre VIII, "Le Transfert" (Paris: Editions du Seuil, 1991). All translations are mine. Henceforth cited as *T*.

reservations. He felt that Claudel's stature is not enhanced by these letters, yet we are assured that he is one of the greatest poets who has ever lived. What drew Lacan to the Trilogy once again was the discussion of the publication of *L'Otage* found in the correspondence. Apparently there were problems because a letter had to be cast for its printing—capital u with a circumflex (Û). No press in France had such a character. Lacan's interest was stimulated by the sign of this missing signifier. He sensed that a rereading of *L'Otage* would be fruitful and would take him far. Such was indeed the case. (*T* 318)[2]

He proceeds with caution, however, warning his students on several occasions that Claudel's values are the values of faith. His theater has the odor of religion which may please or displease his readers and audience. Yet Lacan dismisses the importance of this. Whether one likes Claudel's perspective or not, what counts, we are told, is that he has nonetheless produced a tragedy. The Trilogy is unique. One may disagree with Claudel's conclusions, but the effort must be made to understand him for his entire theatre from *Tête d'Or* to *Le Soulier de satin* (*The Satin Slipper*) is *the* tragedy of desire. (*T* 379)[3]

---

[2]Later on in the seminar, Lacan mentions that he was surprised to discover, on rereading one of the public lectures he gave at the *Collège philosophique* on obsessional neurosis the title of which he is unsure—he thinks it may perhaps have been *Le Mythe du névrosé*, that he had spoken of *Le Père humilié* at that time in the context of a discussion of the function of mythical structures in determining symptoms in the case of the Rat Man. The piece in question is "Le mythe individuel du névrosé" (1953). *Ornicar?* 17/18 (1979): 289-307. Martha Noel Evans' translation appeared as "The Neurotic's Individual Myth," *The Psychoanalytic Quarterly* 48 (1979): 405-25.

[3]It should be noted that Lacan has almost unbounded admiration for Claudel. He is very familiar with his work—his theatre, his poetry, and his correspondence. In his seminar on ethics he reveals that he is also familiar with his prose. He especially appreciates Claudel's insights as an art critic. (*E* 344)

L'Otage (The Hostage)

Lacan begins his study of *L'Otage* by recounting the story. It is a somber tale which takes place during the reign of Napoleon I. The heroine, Sygne de Coûfontaine, is a noblewoman who, for the past 10 years or so, has been engaged in the heroic task of patiently rebuilding the Coûfontaine domain which had been confiscated during the Revolution. Lacan points out that her ties to this domain are in a sense mystical and represent the identity and the very worth of her class. Hers is a feudal allegiance to land and family implying birth rights and caste distinctions. When the action begins, her cousin Georges, who had emigrated, secretly returns accompanied by none other than the Pope, who is quite literally the earthly representative of the heavenly Father in the play. Georges has rescued him from his oppressors. A third character, one who dominates the entire trilogy, is the Baron Toussaint Turelure whose father was a sorcerer and whose mother was Sygne's nurse, in other words, her servant. It is he who was responsible for the massacre of the entire Coûfontaine family during the Revolution and it is now he who wants Sygne's hand in marriage in exchange for the safety of the Pope.

Lacan acknowledges that this peculiar plot, which appears so outdated, could seemingly only appeal to a very restricted audience. Yet he notes the impact, the sense of tragedy, which a cultivated, well-educated, and modern audience feels when witnessing the denouement of *L'Otage*. Lacan sets out to discover what this emotion means. He asserts that the play is one of the greatest in theatrical tradition and that it will be well worth the effort to uncover the mystery of what moves us so deeply in a story which takes the form of a challenge pushed to the extreme of caricature. It has very little to do, he assures us, with the familiar reactions to the suggestion of religious values. (*T* 321)

He begins his analysis by examining the central scene of the drama. Sygne has discovered that her cousin Georges, whom she loves, has been betrayed by his wife and has lost his children. He is bereft of all save his royalist loyalties. In the dialogue which will unleash the tragedy, Sygne and Georges commit themselves to one another before God. It is following this that the saintly Curé Badilon asks her to consider the fact that her refusal of Turelure's proposal will result in the Pope's capture by his enemies. Her acceptance, on the other hand, will produce a divine deliverance, but it will also represent the renunciation of her very being, of her sacred commitment to the man she loves, and of her fidelity to her own family since she would have to marry their exterminator. She is clearly a woman capable of sacrificing her life, but this, as Lacan points out, involves the forfeiture of something worth more to her than her life—it is the forfeiture of her reasons for living, of the very things that determine her being.

Sygne gives in and marries Turelure. The play ends the day of the birth of their child. It is also the day Turelure is to give the keys of the city of Paris to Louis XVIII. Sygne's cousin Georges is present as the king's ambassador. Both he and Turelure are armed. Shots are fired. Sygne saves her husband's life and loses her own by throwing herself into the crossfire. Suicide? Perhaps. In the last scene, prior to her death, we see that she is afflicted with a facial tic. And this is the sign, Lacan tells us, that she has surpassed the limit which Sade himself respected—that of beauty impervious to offense. Lacan feels that this grimace of life which suffers, undermines beauty more than Antigone's grimace of death as she dies suspended from a cord with her tongue hanging out. (*T* 324)

There are two endings to *L'Otage*. In one we witness the entrance of the king and the hideous Turelure receiving a reward for his services. In the other, Sygne, before her death, is exhorted by Badilon. All he obtains is negation, absolute refusal of peace, of abandonment, of surrender to God. Lacan remarks that her destiny, which she cannot accept, surpasses all that can be found in ancient tragedy. It surpasses what was called the function of the evil god by Ricoeur who studied *Antigone* at the same time Lacan did. The evil god of ancient tragedy is tied to humans by the intermediary of *Atè*—folly, delusion, blindness—which he controls and which has a meaning.[4] In *L'Otage* Lacan claims that we are beyond meaning. Sygne's sacrifice only results in the absolute derision of its purpose. The Pope, whom she saves, will be represented, until the end of the trilogy, as an impotent father, and the so-called restoration will be in reality only a fiction, the prolongation of the subverted order. (*T* 325)

Claudel also adds to the second ending a scene in which Turelure himself exhorts Sygne using the motto of her family coat of arms which has defined her life—*Coûfontaine adsum*. He tries to get from her a sign of her acceptance or consent, perhaps in gratitude for the fact that she saved his life. She only answers no. Lacan ponders the significance of such a spectacle being presented to us. The impact is overwhelming. It is the derision of the signifier itself. How can such a thing have emerged from human imagination? What is it about *L'Otage* that touches us, draws us, holds us, and then propels us toward its sequel in the trilogy? Lacan concludes that there is something here for which terminology is lacking. It is beyond Aristotle's terror and pity. It is the image of a desire next to which the only valid reference which remains is Sade. In his analysis of *Antigone* which appears in his *Ethics*, Lacan spoke of a second death which the heroine faced. Here, in *L'Otage*, our heroine is actually asked to embrace this second death. Lacan refers to Sade's topology of tragic destiny in connection with *Antigone*, which does not, as many would have it, go beyond good and evil, but just simply beyond good, to the second limit where the second death is designated by what Lacan calls the

---

[4]In *Myth and Thought Among the Greeks* (Boston: Routledge and Kegan Paul, 1983), 115. Jean Pierre Vernant provides a range of possible interpretations of *atè*, including the following: *atè* is the grandchild of "Nux" (Night) and child of the evil aspect of "Eris," that is "Strife" (94); it is also associated with "aberrations of the mind" (75); moreover, it is "related to Darkness, Scotos. . .an image of the darkness which enshrouds the human spirit suddenly, enfolding it in shadows; finally, *atè* appears as "oblivion and the spirit of error" and also as "criminal waywardness" that leads to "defilement, punishment, and death which result from this" (115). Cited by Mohammad Kowsar in "Lacan's *Antigone*: A Case Study in Psychoanalytical Ethics" in *Critical Theory and Performance*, ed. Janelle G. Reinelt and Joseph R. Roach (Ann Arbor: The University of Michigan Press, 1992), 411. Henceforth cited as *A*.

phenomenon of beauty.[5] Twenty centuries after Christ, Sygne's drama takes us beyond this second limit. (*T* 323)   Lacan claims that Antigone is identical to her destiny or *Atè*, the divine law that sustains her in her trial.   Sygne, on the other hand, in an act of free will, will go against her own will, against all that determines, not only her life, but her very being. Her faith requires that her marriage not be a constraint.   It requires adhesion to the fundamental obligation of marriage, the obligation to love in a union which is freely chosen and indissoluble.

The image of woman has been substituted for the sign of the Christian cross. Lacan is struck by the association of the theme of the cross with the theme of overstepping a limit, of going beyond faith.   This play, ostensibly by a believer, but which many believers have considered blasphemous, is perhaps the sign that a new meaning has been given to human tragedy. (*T* 327)

Sygne's radical refusal is linked to Freud's *Versagung* which implies the

---

[5]Mohammad Kowsar has this to say about Lacan's concept of beauty: "For Lacan ethics and aesthetics are linked by the common denominator of desire and share analogous correspondences. The function of the good consigns to pleasure a limit and a beyond; the function of the 'beautiful' is that which appears beyond the limit set by the good. In the person of Antigone, Lacan can identify for us the dialectics of beauty and desire, in the sense that desire manifests itself in its purest expression as something that is projected beyond human laws. Thus, Lacan reevaluates tragedy by identifying the central conflict of tragic action as 'the effect of beauty on desire.' (*E* 291) This novel discourse does not cancel the technical terms associated with tragedy; in fact, pity and fear still play a role in the dialectics of desire, as does that particular notion of catharsis which is linked to the Dionysian *sparagmos*. But tragedy, for Lacan, is first and foremost a function of desire, and any kind of epiphany, with its concomitant pleasure, can be understood in relationship to a crisis that desire undergoes when faced with the challenge of crossing over 'into another dimension.' (*E* 288) Pleasure is located, according to Lacan, on this side (*deçà*) of 'the fearful center of desire's aspiration,' death—and Freud had said as much—on the other side, beyond (*au-delà*). (*E* 288) Between this side (where pleasure resides) and beyond (the place of certain death) there lies pity and fear. As passions, the functions of pity and fear are to fold back on the central image of desire and to modify the subject's psychic status with a single representation, which is the effect of beauty. Reverberating from Antigone, this sudden effect of beauty designates a 'place' of 'limits.' (*E* 291) Furthermore, by marking a place of limits, Antigone's beauty will structure a relationship between this side and beyond. Beyond lies death; but this side, having experienced the effect of beauty, is no longer here, a place of the living, but a place for a life that not only anticipates death but also partakes in death. As such, the place of pure desire (associated with Antigone) is a zone that is circumscribed by two deaths: 'death encroaching on the domain of life, life encroaching on death' (*E* 291)." (*A* 407) Regarding the second death, we must also keep in mind that Lacan knew very well that for Claudel the second death was perdition. In fact, the Curé Badilon specifically mentions the second death in the play; he calls it sin.

failure to keep a promise, a promise for which everything has been renounced. The *Versagung*, the refusal, which she cannot overcome, becomes what the word implies—*le refus concernant le dit...la perdition* (refusal concerning the said...perdition). We are at the second degree, the deepest reaches of refusal brought about by the word—the promise—and it opens on to the unfathomable. Lacan warns against dismissing this as an extreme, an excess, a paradox of religious madness. He will attempt to demonstrate, on the contrary, that this place of radical refusal is precisely the place where modern man finds himself to the extent that he lacks that religious madness. (*T* 353)

The extreme reached by Oedipus is also surpassed in *L'Otage*. A destiny was imposed on Oedipus determined by the economy of parental structure. What emerges from that, what enters the world at that point, is the implacable play of debt or obligation. Oedipus in the end is only guilty of the charge that he receives from the debt of the *Atè* which precedes him. Lacan reminds us that since then other things have transpired. The Word has been made flesh for us. He came into the world and, contrary to what the Gospel says, Lacan claims that we did indeed recognize and acknowledge him. And we are living out the consequences of that recognition. It is the debt itself which can now be taken from us and it is in this way that we can feel ourselves totally alienated from ourselves. Undoubtedly, the ancient *Atè* made us guilty of this debt, but by renouncing it as we can now do, we are left with an even greater unhappiness produced by the fact that this destiny may no longer be anything. Psychoanalytic experience teaches that we are accountable for the guilt which remains, the guilt which is so palpable in the neurotic. The debt must be paid precisely because the God of destiny is dead.[6]

---

[6] In "Desire and *The Hostage*," (*Theatre Journal* 46.1 [March 1993]) Mohammad Kowsar claims Christian tragedy, in Lacan's view, responded to an ethos that proceeded to bind its subject to law, not by dint of indisputable ordinance, but by fostering a regime of culpability accountable to a shifty Father. He claims that for Lacan the governance of the Father is in no way different from the authority of the Word in the New Testament. (90) He seems not to have grasped that the alienation Lacan points to springs from the fact that with the death of Christ, the death of God, if you will, the debt has been taken from us. We can renounce it, and yet, we are now even more miserable for although we have believed that there is no debt, that there is no reason for guilt, we somehow still cling to it; we cling that which no longer is anything and so we can now be reproached with having

That the God of destiny is dead is at the heart of what Claudel presents to us, according to Lacan. The dead God is represented by that proscribed priest who is the hostage. He is the figure of what was the ancient faith, now at the mercy of politics, prey to those who would use him to restore the monarchy. The counterpart of this reduction of the dead God is that it is the faithful soul who becomes hostage, hostage to this situation where, beyond the end of Christian truth, tragedy is reborn. Everything slips away if the signifier can be captive. Sygne, because she believes, must testify to what she believes. She is caught because of this and is then called to sacrifice to the negation of what she believes. She has been made hostage to negation and suffers because of what is best in her. We have something here which goes further than Job's sufferings and his resignation. Job bears a suffering which he has not merited but the heroine of modern tragedy is asked to take pleasure in the very injustice which horrifies her.

Modern man has become hostage to the Word because he has said to himself, or so that he might say to himself, that God is dead. At that moment the abyss opens where nothing else can be articulated but a negation, a refusal, a no, that tic, that grimace which is the point at which we have to find the mark of the signifier. (*T* 355)

Claudel admits that this play strikes fear even in his own heart. He says it leaves the spectator and the author himself in a painful state of suspense, dissatisfaction, and anguish. He calls the sacrifice inhuman and against nature.[7] As an old man, he wonders how he could have been so ferocious in mid-life when he wrote the Trilogy. The Turelure in him, who is still only too present, responds: "We were young then and we had boiling alcohol in our veins." (*Th*, II, 1425) Yet he would deny that we are here beyond the end of Christian truth. He instead claims that Sygne has merely been called to a particular imitation of Christ who

---

the guilt.

[7] Paul Claudel, *Théâtre de Paul Claudel*, II (Paris: Gallimard, 1965), 1456. Henceforth cited as *Th*.

"became sin for our sakes." As precedent he cites the case of Clotilde who married Clovis and that of Edwige and Jagellon. He is convinced that his audiences would have been less scandalized if Sygne had sacrificed herself to save a fiancé or a natural father.

It was only in his old age that the poet admitted the atrocity of what was asked of Sygne. (*Th*, II, 1417) Yet it is clear that he was never unaware of his own ferocity. When the curate Badilon waits for a response from Sygne after having challenged her to make the terrible sacrifice, he likens himself to Moses contemplating the rock after he had struck it. This comparison is telling for Claudel knew that Moses had sinned in striking the rock. Moses would pay dearly for his excessive zeal. He did not enter the promised land because of it.[8]

In a later commentary on *L'Otage*[9] Lacan adds another dimension to his reading. His context is now the Hegelian dialectic of master and slave. He notes that Sygne is the supreme image of the master. She wished to abandon nothing of her register, the register of the master and the values to which she sacrifices bring her, over and above her sacrifice, no more than the need to renounce, in all its depths, her very being. It is in so far as, through the sacrifice of these values, she is found to renounce her essence, her very being, her most intimate being, that she illustrates, in the end, how much radical alienation of freedom there is in the master himself. This reading is closer to Claudel's own interpretation of his character. He speaks of Sygne's haughty pride and claims that if she had had more generosity she could have created a new race. She proves incapable of renewing the ancient alliance of her class with the people. Her failure demonstrates that the aristocracy did not have the strength to embrace the revolution. (*Th*, II, 1417-26)

---

[8]Nu 20:2-13.

[9]Jacques Lacan, *The Four Fundamental Concepts of Psychoanalysis* (New York: W. W. Norton, 1978), 220.

Le Pain dur (Hard Bread)

Lacan begins his commentary on *Le Pain dur* by discussing the nature of Christian tragedy and the theme of the father. He tells us that when Hegel considers Christian tragedy in the *Phenomenology of the Spirit* he links it with reconciliation and the redemption which resolves the impasse of Greek tragedy. Christian tragedy is at the level of what one might term a divine comedy in which, at the end, all is reconciled in God's providence whether we acknowledge it or not. Lacan cites Kierkegaard and also his own study of *Hamlet* in 1958 as evidence that the Christian era does not end the tragic dimension. There is no trace of reconciliation or redemption in *Hamlet* although one must admit that the presence of the ghost clearly introduces the dimension of Christian faith into the play. Yet it is of the flames of hell and eternal damnation that the ghost of the father gives witness. (*T* 331)

Reflection on the theme of the father and on Freud's question *what is a father*? leads Lacan to observe that the ancient figure of the father was the figure of a king. He suggests that the figure of the divine father in Biblical texts is fertile ground for study. At what point did the God of the Jews become a father? When in history did this happen? When in the prophetic sequence? After posing these questions he remarks that at some point the theme of the father was singularly reduced for it to have taken the obscure form in which it was fixed as the Oedipus complex. He then proceeds to explore what the theme of the father can mean in a tragedy written at a time when, according to Freud, the question of the father has changed profoundly. It is certainly not by accident that Claudel's tragedy is about nothing other than the father.

In *Oedipus* the father has already been killed; in Hamlet the dead father is damned; in Claudel he is humiliated. What does that mean? Who is this humiliated father? Is it the Pope? Lacan believes it to be Toussaint Turelure, the pivotal figure of the centerpiece of the Trilogy, *Le Pain dur*, a play which Lacan finds scandalous coming from the pen of a Catholic author from whom one would expect a depiction of traditional values.[10] Here, instead, we find an extreme derision of the father figure, verging on the abject. Again, all limits are bypassed in a kind of sordidness with Balzacian echoes. (*T* 334)

The play begins with a dialogue between two women. Sygne has been dead for more than 20 years. Turelure is now a sinister, obscene, old man. One of these women, Sichel, is his Jewish mistress; the other, Lumîr, is his son Louis' Polish mistress. Lumîr (to be pronounced *Loum-yir* according to Claudel's instructions) has left Louis in Algeria and has come to ask his father for 20,000 francs, 10,000 of which is money she had lent Louis, money which was not hers. It was the hard-earned savings of Polish immigrants with which she had been entrusted.

The two women, both seductive, as Lacan notes, plot against the greedy Turelure for whom even his son's mistress is not a forbidden object. And here Lacan remarks that this characteristic of the father is a recent addition to the common thematics of certain paternal functions. (*T* 336) He also comments on Claudel's creative reworking of the Oedipal complex.[11] Sichel is not the mother; the mother, Sygne, is dead. Sichel is not the wife either. She is the object of a tyrannical, ambiguous desire. What attaches the father to her, she claims, is a desire to destroy her since he has made her his slave. Turelure was first attracted to her because of her talent as a pianist, and now he forbids her to play. The sudden arrival of Louis, his son, strikes panic in his heart. Turelure obviously sees his son as a repetition of himself, a rival. Lacan feels that this clearly confirms Freud's discoveries. (*T* 337) With the help of Sichel's father, Turelure has been scheming to

---

[10]Again and again Lacan expresses shock at the fact that Claudel is capable of depicting sordid reality. Yet we know that the poet himself identifies with his abject Turelure. In fact, he tells us that his characters are autonomous for the most part. They appear and he himself is surprised by the independence they manifest, by the advice they give him, and by the absolute refusals they sometimes challenge him with. (*Th*, II, 1441)

[11]Claudel himself is quite conscious of this Oedipal dimension. He cites as antecedents of his work Noah, David, Oedipus, and Lear. (*Th*, II, 1418)

deprive his son of his inheritance—the Coûfontaine domain—which Louis officially demanded upon coming of age. But Louis has been warned by Sichel. It is Lumîr, however, who will arm Louis against his father, telling him of the old man's plots and of his advances. Instigated by Sichel, she hatches a scheme which will result in Louis himself assuming the role of father. Lacan does not stop to consider all the intricacies of the plot, although he says they merit our attention, but he does comment on the interplay of the tragic and the farcical found in the play which he considers unique in world literature. He also takes time to note the theme of the historical genesis of colonialism as represented by Louis' exploits in Algeria. He recommends it for further study. (*T* 339)

Louis asks his father for the 20,000 francs which he knows, through Sichel, are actually in his father's pocket. He needs the money so that he can meet his obligations, not only so he can pay his debt to Lumîr, but also to avoid losing what he owns, to avoid becoming a serf on the very land to which his desire drew him—Algeria. It was here that he sought an outlet for the solitude and dereliction produced by the knowledge that his mother Sygne did not want him and that he was a cause of anxiety for his father. In the confrontation, Louis pulls out his guns. He was armed by Lumîr with two pistols, and although she carefully loaded both with real bullets, both will misfire. Yet this does not prevent Turelure from dying. He dies of fright, as expected, since Lumîr had told Louis that one of the weapons contained blanks and that the mere sound of it firing might be sufficient to kill Turelure. If not, then he could use the other with real bullets. Louis fires both simultaneously and learns only later that both were loaded.

When Lumîr comes in and begins searching the body for the money, Louis checks the guns and discovers that they were both really loaded. Lumîr's desire is capable of anything, from the supreme sacrifice of her own life, which we discover later does indeed take place, to a death wish for Louis, her lover. But the parricide has now come into his heritage and will be transformed into another Turelure, another sinister character of whom Claudel will not spare us the caricature. Lacan remarks that Louis becomes an ambassador and assures us that we would be wrong to think that Claudel was not intentionally implicating himself in a strange and ambivalent way with his characters. (*T* 342)[12]

Louis refuses to follow Lumîr although he loves her. He will instead marry his father's mistress, Sichel. At the end of the play we discover that Turelure's financial machinations have placed his wealth in the hands of Ali Habernichts, Sichel's father. It is because Sichel is willing to return it all to Louis that she succeeds in winning him over.[13]

Once again Lacan asks what this strange comedy can mean. After the tragedy of Sygne's sacrifice, we are faced with the total obscurity of a radical derision in *Le Pain dur* at the mid-point or heart of the Trilogy. Lacan begins to answer his own question by pointing out that this play appeared not only in the same century, but actually in the same decade as psychoanalytic thought on the Oedipus complex. (*T* 343) And so we see that Louis, in fact, marries the woman that his father in a sense has given him to marry by the simple fact that she was already his wife. We have here a paradoxical and extreme caricature of the Oedipus complex. It is an outer limit of the Freudian myth which is proposed to us—the obscene old man forces his sons to marry his wives, and this to the exact extent to which he wants to steal their wives from them. This highlights dramatically and expressively in another way what is revealed in the Freudian myth. It doesn't give us a better father, it gives us another scoundrel—Louis, a degraded, degenerate figure of the father. (*T* 357)

---

[12]As we have seen, this is certainly the case. Lacan also mentions the fact that Turelure enjoys modifying names in a derisive manner according to his fancy. Rachel becomes Sichel, which in German means sickle, suggesting the crescent moon and echoing Hugo's *Booz endormi*. Claudel of course has the same habit. Like the old Turelure, he incessantly alters names. (*T* 358)

[13]The Jewish question arises here and also later in *Le Père humilié*. Lacan affirms that as far as he knows no one has ever imputed to Claudel any suspicious attitudes in this regard. The greatness of the old law is not only respected, but exalted, by Claudel throughout his theatre, we are told. Furthermore, Lacan observes that for Claudel *all* Jews are connected with the old law, even those who reject it. The Jew, he adds, gravitates to the sharing by all of the only thing that is real—*la jouissance*. Such is Sichel who has always loved Louis. (*T* 343)

The father is present at the beginning of analytic thought in a form which comedy can well capture, demonstrating all his scandalous attributes. Lacan feels that analytic thought should have articulated a drama. On a contemporary stage one can measure not only the father's criminal character but also the possibility of a decomposition which is caricatural and even abject. But why did this decomposition or caricature became necessary. What accounts for the emergence of this image on humanity's horizon?—if not its consubstantiation with the discovery of the importance of the dimension of desire. (*T* 344)

That what is presented to us in *Le Pain dur* is the myth of Oedipus cannot be doubted, asserts Lacan. He notes that his own distinctive play on words can almost be found in the scene between Louis and his father. Louis in a unique moment seems to demand affection. He says: "Quand même, tu es le père" ("After all, you are the father") and this statement contains a hidden "tuer le père" ("kill the father") which Lumîr's desire suggested to him and which Lacan assures us is not simply a fortuitous linguistic suggestion. (*T* 378)[14]

It is at this moment that the son becomes a man. He becomes the father, yet at the same time he is castrated. His desire for Lumîr will have no outlet, even though it would seem so simple for him merely to return to Algeria with her. But she does not want to go with him. She provokes the parricide and then she goes off toward her own destiny which is the destiny of a desire, the kind of desire that only one of Claudel's characters can have.[15] She drops Louis to pursue what is clearly indicated as a death wish. And the result is this interesting variation on the Oedipal myth—she turns him over, not to the mother, but to his father's wife. The rejected,

---

[14]Incredibly, this phrase is nowhere to be found in the text. Lacan's admiration of Claudel has led him to mar his otherwise careful reading with a fanciful fabrication. It is an astonishing attempt to create common ground between himself and the poet. Lacan's inventiveness also finds another, perhaps more legitimate convergence with Claudel which he attributes to cabalistic geomancy. He recognizes in the substitution of a *y* for an *i* in Sygne's name, his own S by which he demonstrates how the imposition of the signifier on man is both what marks him and what disfigures him (*T* 352).

[15]Claudel calls her a new Antigone. (*Th*, II, 1444).

unwanted son is reestablished. He will recreate the defeated father. In castration, Lacan tells us, one is deprived of one's desire and in exchange, one is given to another. Lumîr sees it clearly: Louis must marry his father's mistress. The structure here is remarkable. It would seem hardly worth noting because it has become so familiar, but Lacan insists that it is rarely expressed in this manner.

In the first instance, Sygne, too, was deprived of her desire and in exchange she is put on the market. All is taken from her and in exchange for what is taken from her she herself is given to what she most despises. (*T* 380)

Claudelian drama permits Lacan to once again place the question of castration at the center of the problem of the father. He considers castration identical to the constitution of the subject of desire as such. It is identical to the phenomenon which makes the object of desire or lack—desire is lack—identical to the instrument of desire itself—the phallus. On any level, not only the genital, the object of desire, to be characterized as such, must come to the same symbolic place that the instrument of desire, the phallus, fills—in so far as it fulfills the function of signifier. And why does this instrument fulfill the function of signifier? Precisely in order to fill the symbolic place—the place of the father already dead. It is of course the father who articulates the law. But law to be instituted as law requires as antecedent the death of the one who supported it. It is at this level that the phenomenon of desire is produced. A radical gap appears. This is found in Claudel whether he realized it or not. And the fact that he could not suspect in what context his work would one day be inscribed makes his findings more convincing, just as it was thoroughly convincing to see Freud enunciate in advance the laws of metaphor and metonymy in his work. (*T* 345)

The explosion which produces the configuration of desire decomposes in three phases which can be distinguished in the generations. To situate the composition of desire in a subject it is not necessary to go back to Adam. Three generations suffice. In the first, the mark of the signifier. Sygne tragically illustrates this as an extreme example in Claudel's composition. She is driven to the destruction of her being and torn from all her attachments of fidelity and faith. In the second a child appears. Those who speak, those who are marked by the word, engender. Louis in the second generation is the object which has been totally rejected, the undesired object. The third generation is the only real one. The others are artificial decompositions, antecedents of the only one that counts. Here we see how desire constitutes itself between the mark of the signifier and the passion of the partial object. (*T* 346-47)

Claudel himself recognizes a similar configuration. He tells us that like the Greek tragedians, he, in fact, believed that the narrow limits of one generation do not suffice to imprison the mysterious intentions of Moïra. His entire childhood was cradled with tales of ancient crimes, mixed with obscure sacrifices, whose pathetic outcomes he slowly saw develop before his eyes from the lips of an old servant. He saw the children in the ancient legend, as in official history, take up this thread of the Fates from the hands of their dying parents in order to transmit it finally to some chosen one in this mystical saga. And this occurred in the third generation of which the Scripture speaks, in which the *meaning* of the arcanum is finally realized, the meaning of the underlying counsel inherent to a sequel which carries with it something like the fatality of a musical phrase. The events then, suddenly amalgamated one to the other, take on the value of a teaching and an anecdote; the saga is transformed into a parable. (*Th*, II, 1455)[16]

---

[16]It would seem then that the meaninglessness of Sygne's sacrifice was only apparent. Its meaning will become evident in the third generation.

Le Père humilié (The Humiliated Father)

What does Pensée de Coûfontaine, daughter of Louis and Sichel, granddaughter of Sygne, and heroine of *Le Père humilié,* mean? Lacan will investigate Pensée's meaning as though she were a living personage. He is concerned with her desire and the very thought of desire, "la pensée même du désir." His will not be an allegorical interpretation, but the ambiguity of the names the poet gave his characters seems to legitimate an interpretation of them as moments of the incidence of the symbolic on living flesh itself. (*T* 352) What desire can be reborn in a feminine figure who responds to the figure of Sygne from the radical position of Sygne's refusal and sacrifice? This is Lacan's question.

He begins his commentary by affirming that Pensée is undeniably seductive and is clearly presented to us as an object of desire. But why? What does she counterbalance? What does she compensate for? Will something be due her because of Sygne's sacrifice? Will she represent some sort of exemplary figure, a recognition of the faith which was for an instant eclipsed? On the contrary, responds Lacan. She is a free-thinker who only has one passion—that of justice, not of any justice, but of a justice which goes beyond the demands of beauty itself. It is absolute justice that she desires, the justice that inspires the revolution which serves as backdrop for this third drama. Here, Claudel is as far as he can be from the preaching that one would expect of a man of faith. (*T* 357)

We find then in the offspring of Louis and Sichel the rebirth of what was put aside in *Le Pain dur,* the same absolute desire which animated Lumîr. (*Loum-yir—lumière*—light, suggests Lacan.) Pensée also incarnates her mother's dark and patient search for light. She will become the incarnate object of the desire for light and as such she could only be imagined by the poet as blind. Yet Lacan wonders what Claudel could possibly want with this incarnation of the object—the partial object, the object in so far as it is the resurgence and the effect of a parental constellation—a blind girl who appears before us in the third play in the most moving manner. (*T* 358)

We are in Rome on the eve of its capture by Garibaldi's followers. Pensée appears at a masked ball. The festivities also serve as farewell to a Polish nobleman who is about to be dispossessed of all his belongings. He wears on his arm a cameo of Lumîr who, we discover, has met a sad end. Pensée moves about in this setting as though she were sighted. No one guesses that she is blind although the audience knows that to be the case. Orian and Orso Homodarmes are the two male protagonists.[17] Orso, the younger brother, loves Pensée. Pensée loves Orian. Why him, since she can barely distinguish the two brothers' voices? Perhaps only because he is inaccessible.

Lacan begins to sketch an answer to his questions concerning Pensée by noting that a sort of sublime figure of modesty seems to guard her. She cannot see herself being seen and therefore seems protected against the gaze which would unveil. Nothing can be shown to her which would submit her to the other, *le petit autre*, and one cannot spy upon her without being struck with blindness like Actaeon or being torn to pieces by ones own desires. As Lacan points out, the word does not elicit sight. The word is by its nature blindness. One sees oneself being seen and one hides. But one does not hear oneself being heard. Only the madman who hallucinates hears himself being heard. One must be in the place of the Other to hear oneself heard. Lacan concludes that what Claudel means with Pensée is that all the soul has to do is close its eyes to the world to become all that the world lacks and the most desirable object in the world. Lacan has no doubts that Claudel speaks of the soul. Psyche who can no longer light the lamp draws to herself the being of Eros who is lack. The myth of Poros and Penia is here reborn in the form of spiritual blindness, for we are told that Pensée incarnates the figure of the Synagogue as she is represented in the Cathedral of Rheims, blindfolded. Orian, on the other hand, is someone who can give; he is superabundance. But he is also a

---

[17] Although not noted by Lacan, Orian and Orso are nephews of the Pope.

form of refusal. He is unwilling to give Pensée his love because he claims that his gifts are needed elsewhere in God's vineyard. What he does not understand is that what is demanded in love is not one's *poros*, one's abundance, not even, as he says, his joy. It is rather what he does not have. Orian is a saint, and Lacan is struck by the manner in which Claudel, through him, shows us the limits of sainthood. Yet desire here is stronger than sainthood itself. Orian will succumb to Pensée. (*Th*, II, 361)[18] In the last scene of the drama a pregnant Pensée is under the protection of her mother. She receives a visit from Orso who comes to deliver a final message from his dead brother. It was his wish that Pensée and Orso would wed. Lacan observes that in this scene Pensée is the sublime object positioned as substitute for *la Chose* whose nature is not far from that of woman, although, he says, in close proximity woman always proves to be yet something else. (It is in *Partage de midi* [*Break of Noon*] that Lacan feels Claudel has created a woman, Ysé, who strongly resembles what woman is.) (*T* 362)

We are in the presence of the object of a desire and what Lacan wants to demonstrate, what he claims is inscribed in her image, is that it is a desire which, at this level of privation or detachment, only castration separates, although quite radically, from any natural desire. What we have here then is a figure of woman deified in order to become once again the crucified woman. From the Princess in *Tête d'Or*, to Sygne herself, to Ysé in *Partage de midi*, to the figure of Dona Prouhèze in *Le Soulier de satin* (*The Satin Slipper*), all of Claudel's heroines follow this pattern. And what does this figure of woman carry within herself? — an infant. Pensée's child will stir for the first time when she absorbs the soul of Orian who is dead. Pensée covers herself with the wings of her cloak over the basket of flowers that Orso has sent and which we discover contains the eviscerated heart of her lover

---

[18]Pensée tells us that she went to him silently in the night on the battlefield. He was fighting in the Pope's army. We surmise that he was killed shortly thereafter.

Orian.[19] She breathes in his soul. It is this transmission, this fusion of souls, which is presented as the supreme aspiration of love. Orso, who knows that he will soon join his brother, is the vehicle of that fusion. Lacan admits that one is tempted to think of Orso as a ridiculous figure ready to be husband in name only to a woman who doesn't love him simply to provide legitimacy to his brother's child and protection to its mother. But, he notes, in reality the place he occupies is the very one to which the spectator is drawn. This fantasm is proposed to his desire revealing the structure of this desire and revealing too the magnetic force in woman which draws man, and not necessarily upward. This force is threefold, and if possessed, can only represent man's destruction. (*T* 363-4)

There is always in love some delight in death, but in a death which cannot be inflicted on oneself. There are four terms here which Lacan tells us are represented in man—the two brothers, *a* and *a'*—the spectator or subject in so far as he understands nothing—and the figure of the Other incarnated in the woman.[20] Among these four elements all sorts of variations of death inflicted are possible, among which one could enumerate the most perverse forms of desire. Here it is the most ethical scenario which is presented since we are dealing with an authentic, completed man who affirms and maintains his virility—Orian, who pays the price with his death.

Thus the poet accomplishes his purpose. After the drama of subjects as pure

---

[19]This theme of love linked to death was also discussed in connection with *Le Pain dur*. There Lacan mentioned the sacrificed lover as seen in Stendhal's *Le Rouge et le noir*. He alludes to the story of the real life La Mole whose severed head was taken by a woman and the imaginary Mlle de la Mole who will embrace Julien's severed head. (*T* 341) Claudel himself speaks of an Italian legend that Browning recounted as having been what inspired Stendhal. (*Th*, II, 1454) It is also interesting to note that the church of Brangues, where Paul Claudel's chateau is located, was the site of the crime depicted in Stendhal's novel.

[20]The figure four was also noted by Lacan in connection with *Le Pain dur*. He speaks of "une sorte de singulière partie carrée" ("a sort of singular game for four players") comprised of Turelure, Louis, Sichel, and Lumîr (*T* 337). It is the *partie carrée* of the card game whist which Lacan has often evoked to designate the structure of the analytic position. (*T* 338) The figure four and its importance in Claudel's thought was examined by me in *Woman and the Feminine Principle in the Works of Paul Claudel*.

victims of *logos*, of language, he shows us what becomes of desire. And to do that, he makes this desire visible in the form of a woman—that terrible subject, Pensée de Coûfontaine. She merits her name, Pensée, for she is thought on desire. The love she expresses, love of the other, is fixed in her and she becomes the object of desire.

The long path of tragedy ends with this topology. Lacan notes that as in all processes and all progress in human articulation, it is only after the fact that one understands where the lines traced in the traditional past converge and what they announce and reveal. All through Euripides' tragedy we find, like a wound which torments, the relationship to desire. Lacan is convinced that what one calls Euripides' misogyny, which is a kind of aberration or folly that seems to strike all of his poetry, can only be grasped when one considers what it became after it passed through the sublimation of the Christian tradition. (*T* 364)

Of what use is Claudelian mythology? This is Lacan's final question. He begins to formulate an answer by reviewing the structuralist articulation of myth. Taking a myth in its totality, its *epos* or story, one can construct a model solely constituted by a series of oppositional connotations—for example, in the myth of Oedipus, the father-son relationship. But the myth doesn't stop there. There are subsequent generations and if we are really dealing with a myth, these generations are not simply a succession, the young replacing the old for the sake of continuity. There is a significant coherence between the first constellation and the one that follows. The challenge is to detect the rules that lend rigor; a rigor, however, that must be contained in the play of the myth. In the function of the myth, transformations occur according to certain rules which provide a revelatory value that creates superior configurations or particular cases which are illuminating. In other words, myth contains the same fecundity as math. (*T* 373)

Lacan maintains that one cannot engage in analysis without encountering the function of myth. From the very beginning of analysis, in *Traumdeuting*, Freud supports his argument with a reference to myth, the Oedipus myth. And although the goal of analysis is not the introduction of the subject to his destiny, which would put the analyst in the position of a demiurge, yet, Lacan asserts that if there is anything that the Freudian discovery has taught, it is to see in symptoms a figure which somehow relates to the figure of destiny. This was not known before; now it is known and knowing it makes a difference. The fact of knowing or not knowing is essential to the figure of destiny and Lacan claims that myths confirm this. (*T* 375)

Myths are developed figures that can be related, not to language, but to the implication of a subject caught in language—and to complicate things, caught in the play of words. From the relationship of the subject to a signifier, figures develop where one can discern—necessary points, irreducible points, major points, points of intersection. These points, once discerned, permit analysts to reconcile the real function of trauma with their experience of development. Traumas can then be defined as events which situate themselves in a certain position in this structure of points and there, they take on the signifying value that the subject attaches to them. This is what makes an event traumatic and it is from this that the interest in returning to the experience of myths arises.

Lacan feels that there is some problem with Greek myth owing to the many existing variants and its uncertain origin. As we know, he has recourse to *Hamlet* to illustrate what happens to the Oedipal conflict when knowledge penetrates the interior of the myth. Unlike the father in *Oedipus*, Hamlet's father *knows* who killed him and why. It is this knowledge, which he passes on to Hamlet, that will unleash the tragedy. (*T* 377) At the origin of neurosis, Freud said from his first works, there is a *Versagung*, not a frustration as some have interpreted it, but, as we have seen, something closer to a refusal. It is obvious, declares Lacan, that this untranslatable *Versagung* is only possible at the level of *sagen*, in so far as *sagen* is not simply the operation of communication, but of the spoken, the emergence of the signifier as such in so far as it permits the subject to refuse himself. This original, primordial refusal, this power of refusal is impossible to escape in analysis. It is important then to understand this *Versagung* and here is where the Claudelian myth is useful, for Lacan found in *L'Otage* a spectacular way of imaging the phenomenon of *Versagung*.

On the other hand, in *Le Pain dur*, which is clearly about the myth of Oedipus, there is an exemplary structural decomposition of the function of what the mother represents in Freudian myth—a sort of empty space, a center of aspiration, a vertiginous point for the libido. Louis kills his father, takes his place only to experience castration—the object of his desire, Lumîr, is denied him. He is then given, not the mother, Sygne, who is dead; but instead, his father's wife, Sichel, herself rehabilitated by the incidence of desire. She, in turn, rehabilitates him, reestablishes him, recreates with him the father who had been defeated. The structure is what is important here. The subject is denied his or her desire and in exchange is put on the market and passes into the general auction. And wasn't this precisely what happened at the beginning, at the first level, in another form, to Sygne? Yet the effects of becoming subject to the law are not summed up in a person being deprived of everything desired and, in exchange, being given over to the elaboration of the thread that ties the generations together. For one still owes something if, at the end of the action which ties the generations together, there remains a debit which is not matched by a corresponding credit. (*T* 380-81)[21]

Finally, we see what psychoanalysis can learn by exploring Claudel's theatre. Lacan explains why it is, in fact, necessary for analysts to explore the remarkable extremes present there. These extremes are the points of the sundering of terms whose intersection brings about the effects that analysts must deal with—those of neurosis. These points must be explored if analysts want their activity to be properly situated and oriented, if they want to respond to what is in the other, the one they accompany in the transference. Extremes touch me,

---

[21]It should be noted in this context that Claudel felt his work was unfinished. He dreamed of providing a conclusion or solution to the Trilogy—a fourth drama. All he could sense concerning it was that it would revolve around a very old Pensée who would play the role of a Pythia. She would unite in herself the explanation of all past agitation while at the same time representing an opening to the future. (*Th*, II, 1452) We should say that although the figure four would have been introduced with the proposed conclusion, the tripartite configuration would have been left in tact, since it would still have been in the third generation, with Pensée, that the drama culminated.

someone said. Analysts must also touch them— even if it is just for a moment—to be able to know exactly what their place should be when the subject is on the only path to which they had to lead him, the one where he must articulate his desire. (*T* 365)

CHAPTER 5

TRAGIC WISDOM

An Introduction to Gabriel Marcel's Thought

Let us now turn our attention to another great reader of Paul Claudel—Gabriel Marcel (1889-1973) in order to further explore the instruction of philosophy by tragedy. We will begin by considering the broad outlines of his thought and then examine his views on tragic wisdom.

Generally speaking, for Gabriel Marcel modern man has lost his awareness of the sense of the ontological—that is, the sense of being. If ontological needs worry modern man at all, it is only dully, as an obscure impulse.[1] The thirst for being, the ontological exigency, is the search for a meaning in life, for a consistency within, for a "plenitude which is opposed to the internal void in a functionalized world and opposed to the overwhelming monotony of a society where people appear more and more as simple specimens less and less distinguishable one from the other."[2] Marcel notes that the ontological need, the need of being, is exhausted in exact proportion to the breaking up of the personality on the one hand and, on the other, to the triumph of the category of the "purely natural" and the consequent

---

[1]Gabriel Marcel, *The Philosophy of Existence* (Plainview, NJ: Books for Libraries Press, 1969), 1. Henceforth cited as *PE*.

[2]René Davignon, *Le Mal chez Gabriel Marcel* (Paris: Editions du Cerf, 1985) 34. Translation mine. Henceforth cited as *Mal*.

atrophy of the faculty of wonder. (*PE* 4) The more the sense of the ontological tends to disappear, the more unlimited become the claims of the mind to a kind of cosmic governance precisely because it is less and less capable of examining its own credentials for the exercise of such dominion. (*PE* 19)

It appears today more than doubtful that it is possible for human beings, whoever they may be, to discover or to identify a certain kernel within which could be designated as the essential self. And it must be acknowledged that this kind of disintegration of the self is like an indirect invitation to all sorts of interventions and intrusions of society, in whatever forms these may take.[3] Marcel feels it can never be too strongly emphasized that the crisis which the West is undergoing today is a metaphysical one. For him, there is probably no more dangerous illusion than that of imagining that some readjustment of social or institutional conditions could suffice of itself to appease a contemporary sense of disquiet which rises, in fact, from the very depths of our being. (*Mass* 37) The ontological need cannot be completely silenced and certainly not by an arbitrary dictatorial act which mutilates the life of the spirit at its roots. (*Mass* 9) Being, we are told, is—or should be—necessary. For Marcel, it is impossible that everything should be reduced to a play of successive appearances which are inconsistent with each other—"a tale told by an idiot."

But what exactly *is* being, one might ask. Marcel admits that it is extremely difficult to define the word "being." He suggests that being is what withstands—or what would withstand—an exhaustive analysis bearing on the data of experience and aiming to reduce them step by step to elements increasingly devoid of intrinsic or significant value. (He believes an analysis of this kind is attempted in the theoretical works of Freud.) (*PE* 4-5) Being is what satisfies; being is eternal, what

---

[3]Gabriel Marcel, *Man Against Mass Society* (Lanham, MD: University Press of America, Inc., 1985), 293. Henceforth cited as *Mass*.

does not disappoint.[4] Being and life do not then coincide. As Marcel says his life and, by reflection, all life may appear as forever inadequate to something which we carry within, which in a sense we are, but which reality rejects and excludes. (*PE* 14) The principle of whatever it is that we mean by value, can only be *being*. (*Mass* 264) Yet, he warns that we should not lose ourselves in abstract discussions about the intrinsic characteristics of being—as if being were a *thing*, capable of being contrasted with other things, which are only its appearances and manifestations. Being is, quite fundamentally, not something which one can discuss. We can discuss only that which is *not* being and thus, indirectly and humbly, map and mark out the tracks that lead towards being. (*Mass* 173) As Xavier Tilliette remarks, Marcel's reflection intuits and explores being in a distant intimacy, in the depths, as elasticity, detente, permeability, openness, presence, above all, presence; and with the aid of less discrete categories such as plenitude, fulfillment, living peace, fidelity, and creative witness. (*Pc* 34)

Granted the traditional distinction between philosophies of being and philosophies of liberty, clearly Marcel's spontaneous tendency was toward the former. (*PE* 24) For he considers that it is indeed with being that philosophical reflection should concern itself, as all the great philosophers of the past have, and as even in our century Germany's most profound thinker, Heidegger, has.[5] Marcel thought that what Heidegger's position and his own had most fundamentally in common was the sacred sense of being, the conviction that being is a sacral reality. This seems to him extraordinarily important. (We shall examine some commonalities between Heidegger and both Claudel and Marcel in Chapter 6.)

Marcel's effort can perhaps best be described as an attempt to establish a concept which precludes all equation of being with *Ding* while upholding the

---

[4]Xavier Tilliette, *Philosophes contemporains* (Paris: Desclée de Brouwer, 1962) 34. Translation mine. Henceforth cited as *Pc*.

[5]Gabriel Marcel, *Pour une sagesse tragique et son au-delà* (Paris: Plon, 1968) 32. Translation mine. Henceforth cited as *St*.

ontological, yet without going back to the category of substance which he regarded with profound mistrust. (*PE* 95) It should also be added that he considered the Cartesian position to be inseparable from a form of dualism which he unhesitatingly rejects. To raise the ontological problem is to raise the question of being as a whole, of oneself seen as a totality. (*PE* 7)

For him, the fact of being human cannot be thought without reference to being. However, for the distinction which he finds highly suspicious between *l'Être* and *l'Étant*, he proposes to substitute that of *Light* and what is *enlightened by it*. Naturally, by Light no physical agent is designated. When we understand, either gradually or suddenly, what at first seemed obscure to us, we are enlightened and this is as true for the blind person as for the clairvoyant. (*St* 304). Light is conceived as the ultimate ontological given—a given which is at the same time *giving*, and it is in that that it is ultimate. (*St* 306) He speaks of his program of substituting for being the light, the illumining, and for *a* being, the illumined. (*St* 243)

He links presence to being and being to mystery and when discussing the difference between mystery and problem, he explains that a mystery is a problem which encroaches upon its own data, invading them, as it were, and thereby transcending itself as a simple problem. (*PE* 8) But he notes that there is no real hope of establishing an exact frontier between problem and mystery, for in reflecting on a mystery we tend inevitably to degrade it to the level of a problem. This is particularly clear in the case of evil. (*PE* 9) He further explains that mystery is not what we do not understand (comprehend) but instead what comprehends (includes) us. "Mystery is something in which I find myself engaged." (*PC* 20)

The internal dimension of ontological presence or of mystery, is intersubjectivity. We learn that the bond that attaches existence to being, is the "intersubjective nexus. " So long as I remain in my autonomy, my alterity; so long as the other is other to me, a him or her rather than a you—we are in the realm of the triadic and the access to being is obstructed, existence betrayed. (*Mal* 53) "The subjective, is the intersubjective." (*Pc* 35) He feels there is authentic depth only where a communion can be effectively realized; it will never exist between individuals centered on themselves, and as a result hardened; nor in the midst of the masses in that state. Thus the most authentic philosophical thought is "a metaphysics of *we are* in opposition to a metaphysics of *I think*." With "the direct experience of that rush of being" that it calls forth, intersubjectivity reveals itself as an undeniable ontological sign. (*Mal* 53)

Marcel proceeds to argue that the non-objective character of presence does not imply the merely subjective, but that it does imply the intersubjective. He defines the intersubjective as an openness, in the Bergsonian sense of the "open" and the "closed" which he claims leads to a "philosophy of light." For Marcel, intersubjectivity is the fact of being together in the light. It is in this area that Marcel philosophizes, an area which is sometimes very difficult to grasp, an area which is neither objective nor subjective but transcends these categories. It is here that Marcel's use of the term "mysterious" in regard to this communication of two persons, open and attentive to each other, begins to take on definition.[6]

Tilliette points to the fact that the axial approach then goes from existence to being through intersubjectivity. The intersubjective salvages the world of things and people and, to a certain degree, it salvages history. (*Pc* 38) The intersubjective is not, however, the extension of a privileged experience of friendship or of love, it is the interior stuff of the world. (*Pc* 35) The metaphysical is your neighbor. (*Pc* 36) Davignon notes that the search for veritable being and participation in the transcendental are only possible if one opens oneself to intersubjectivity. (*Mal* 52) From the moment when we try to pose ourselves as an absolute, that is, when we try to liberate ourselves from every relationship, from any reference to another than oneself, from that moment we can only in the last analysis destroy ourselves, or rather, what in fact amounts to the same thing, wind up in an idolatry which takes as an object, an abstraction such as class or race, that is something incomparably

---

[6]Denis P. Moran, *Gabriel Marcel: Existentialist, Philosopher, Dramatist, Education* (Lanham, MD: University Press of America, 1992), 13. Henceforth cited as *Edu*.

inferior to that which we want to free ourselves from. (*Mal* 47)   The more we estrange ourselves from our neighbor, the more we are lost in a night in which we can no longer even distinguish being from non-being. (*Mass* 264)

From another, but connected, perspective, it might be said, as Ricoeur does, that Marcel was the one who brought "absolute presence" back to the level of feeling itself. He took the body, rather than language, as the primary focus of his reflection on existence. Ricoeur feels that this should not be forgotten at a time when French philosophy is suffering from a kind of fascination with the problems of language. In joining a criticism of sensation as message to his criticism of the body as instrument, he claims Marcel opened the way to a philosophy of the body-subject, and gave philosophy the means for thinking embodiment.[7] It is the reflection on one's body and on sensation that led Marcel to think that if he, a human being, existed, it was to the extent that he had a body. Through the intermediary of his body he engaged in relationships that cannot in any way be reduced to those that scientific thought determines. (*St* 264) Moran points out that Marcel took issue with the neo-Thomists precisely because of their position on the body. (*Edu* 102)[8]

As Xavier Tilliette notes correctly, Gabriel Marcel then avoided the danger of spiritualisms, of progressive disincarnation. His ontology of intimacy and of light is penetrated with a dense reality, planted in the midst of temporal earth. For the spiritual is itself carnal. Existence is irrevocable, in its depth, in its harshness; it is a destiny that no will can anticipate; it is an "immense consensus." (*Pc* 38)

In this connection Paul Ricoeur observes that Marcel's reflections on "feeling" and on "receiving" in the *Metaphysical Journal* really inaugurated a kind of analysis which was to have great success in the French philosophy of sensation

---

[7]Gabriel Marcel, *Tragic Wisdom and Beyond including Conversations between Paul Ricoeur and Gabriel Marcel*, trans. Stephen Jolin and Peter McCormick (Evanston: Northwestern University Press, 1973), 222. Henceforth cited as *R*.

[8]Marcel remarks: "Without my realizing it exactly, at least at the beginning, that research was oriented toward the incarnated God, toward that God which gave himself existence in becoming man like me." (*St* 264-65)

and that of existence. Sensation was no longer just the business of psychophysiology. According to Marcel, sensation testified to our participation in existence, our participation in the world of existing things. When Marcel criticized the conception of sensation as a message passing between one thing and another, between a transmitter and a receiver, according to Ricoeur, he laid the foundation of what Merleau-Ponty and others later called phenomenology of perception. (*R* 222)

The dynamic of Marcel's philosophy, taken as a whole, can then be seen as an obstinate and untiring battle against the spirit of abstraction. (*Mass* 1) We must, however, distinguish between the notion of abstraction as such, and the spirit of abstraction. He has this to say about the distinction:

> Abstraction, as such, is a mental operation to which we must have recourse if we are seeking to achieve a determinate purpose of any sort. Psychologists have demonstrated with perfect clarity the close internal link between abstraction and action. To abstract, in a word, is to make a preliminary clearing of the ground, and of course this clearing of the ground can appear the strictly reasonable thing to do. This means that the human mind must retain a precise and distinct awareness of those methodical omissions which are necessary if an envisaged result is to be obtained. But it can happen that the mind, yielding to a sort of fascination, ceases to be aware of these prior conditions that justify abstraction and deceives itself about the nature of what is, in itself, nothing more than a method, one might almost say nothing more than an expedient. The spirit of abstraction is not separable from this contempt for the concrete conditions of abstract thinking. I would even say that it *is* this contempt. Perhaps it would not be misleading to say that the spirit of abstraction can in certain respects be regarded as a transposition of the attitudes of imperialism to the mental plane. Possibly Baron Seillière, that little-read philosopher, has seen this as clearly as anyone. As soon as we accord to any category, isolated from all other categories, an

arbitrary primacy, we are victims of the spirit of abstraction....This
operation, of arbitrarily isolating a category, is not really essentially
an intellectual one....We ought to refer ourselves to the exhaustive
analyses of Nietzsche and, more especially, of Scheler, which throw
so much light on the part played by resentment in such reductive
operations....*'This* is only *that...This* is nothing other than *that*', and
so on: every depreciatory reduction of this sort has its basis in
resentment, that is to say, in passion, and at bottom it corresponds to
a violent attack directed against a sort of integrity of the real, an
integrity to which only a resolutely concrete mode of thinking can
hope to do justice. But what we should also notice is that this
depreciatory reduction implies on the other side of the medal a
factitious exaltation of the residual element which the victim of the
spirit of abstraction is claiming to preserve in its purity, having
sacrificed to it what have been defined as mere appearances or mere
superstructures. (*Mass* 156-57)

We saw in Chapter 3, with Nussbaum's commentary on Aristotle, that belief is the
ground of feeling, now we see how feeling can be the ground of thought. Marcel
notes that the element of resentment in human nature is profoundly linked to a
tendency to conceptual dissociation which lies at the opposite pole to the element of
admiration. (*Mass* 158) When he was still very young he grasped the truth that it is
impossible to build true peace on abstractions. (*Mass* 3) As Tilliette remarks,
Marcel distrusts systems of philosophy of whatever kind for there is no system that
does not involve the temptation to declare *a priori* that this or that difficulty is to be
judged unimportant and consequently set aside. (*Pc* 88)

Marcel suggests that the spirit of abstraction is a kind of disease of the
intelligence, yet he acknowledges that this formulation is not really accurate since,
as we have seen, he believes the spirit of abstraction has its origins in the passions,
not the mind. (*Mass* 162) It is passion, not intelligence, which forges the most
dangerous abstractions. He warns too that abstractions are not inoperative: they

contain infinite possibilities for disorder. There is a real connection between horror and abstraction and collective violence. (*Mal* 158)

Marcel's battle against the spirit of abstraction resulted in a method which consisted in taking a concrete example from contemporary history and trying to see what light that example could project on the problem he had posed for himself, rather than starting from an abstract analysis of a notion. (*St* 119) For him, thinking that does not deal seriously with examples always runs the risk of losing itself, of letting itself be deluded by a kind of antecedent linguistic structure. Giving an example was a way of justifying himself to himself, and also of proving to his interlocutor that he is speaking of something, that his words were not empty. Examples served as a kind of irrigation. (*St* 235-36) We recall here Nussbaum's cautionary remarks, noted in Chapter 3, regarding what is suppressed in the philosophical works of the type most familiar in the Anglo-American tradition which do not focus intently on the stories of concrete characters because of systemic considerations.

For Marcel all reflection worthy of the name, that is to say, all reflection conscious of the urgent inner need which is its most secret spring of action, must be exercised for the sake of the concrete, on behalf of the concrete. (*Mass* 159) Philosophy should approach concrete life and reestablish the ties that the spirit of abstraction as well as ideology seem, on the contrary, to try to break wherever they can. (*Mal* 159) And it is, as Ricoeur observes, the problem of intersubjectivity, the problem of others, that ceaselessly brought him toward the inexhaustible wealth of the concrete. It is the act of *recognizing* others which incessantly leads us to experience and makes experience a test. (*R* 254)

Concerning the concrete Marcel tells us that one might be tempted to suppose that it is what is given at first, that it is what our thinking must start from. But, we learn, nothing could be more false than such a supposition: and he points out that here Bergson is at one with Hegel. What is given us to start with is a sort of unnamed and unnameable confusion. It is only by going through and beyond the process of scientific abstraction that the concrete can be regrasped and reconquered.

The problem of peace can be stated in somewhat analogous terms. There is no more dangerous illusion than that of supposing peace to be a kind of preliminary, given state; what is given is something which is not even war, but which contains war in a latent condition. Peace is, in fact, the most difficult of the states to which we can raise ourselves, the supreme elevation. (*Mass* 160) There is a primary reflection which, roughly speaking, is purely analytical and which consists, as it were, in dissolving the concrete into its elements. Reason, then, exploits and transforms —and sometimes also reduces and dissolves, the latter in the case where its exercise becomes purely critical. (*Can* reason ever really *give* us anything? he asks.) (*Mass* 253) Then there is an inverse movement, a movement of retrieval, which consists in becoming aware of the partial and even suspect character of the purely analytical procedure. This reflective movement tries to reconstruct, but now at the level of thought, that concrete state of affairs which had previously been glimpsed in a fragmented or pulverized condition. It is this secondary reflection which he claims is at work in all his philosophical writings, starting from the moment when he truly became fully conscious of his task. (*R* 235) Secondary reflection is recuperative, or if you like, synthetic. It is based on being, not on intuition, on an assurance which is identified with what we call our soul. (*St* 33)

Xavier Tilliette remarks that like Socrates, the ambulant philosopher, Gabriel Marcel, the thinker, is "the *homo viator* par excellence." To harmonious structure which seems to be satisfied with itself, Gabriel Marcel prefers questions and tireless movement that ventilates thought. (*Pc* 10) It is the term "neo-Socratism" which seems an appropriate descriptor since it emphasizes the central role interrogation plays in his thought and the fact that often his primary concern was to find an adequate way to pose problems before attempting to solve them. (*R* 252) He believed that the essential function of the philosopher was that of sowing seeds which can hardly be exercised anywhere but in the intimacy of dialogue, *inter paucos*. Once again the lesson of Socrates. As Davignon notes, Marcel was a watchful philosopher, who tried to struggle without pause "against a sleep that, at the level of spirit, can affect very different forms. The sleep of habit, of prejudice, of dogmatism." Reacting also "against everything that can be oppressive in moralism," Marcel "formulates neither duty nor rule; he doesn't even give any advice. But he is an ethical thinker, in the sense that all his work, dramatic or reflective, aims at awakening the powers in us that have taken the part of being." Far from wanting to play the "prophet," the "iconoclast" or the "Philosopher with a capital letter," he knows, on the contrary, how essential questioning, disquiet and humility are at the center of existential thought. (*Mal* 163-64)

Tilliette is right in saying that Marcel conceives of philosophy above all as a search, with what that word implies of the cautionary, the meticulous and the circumspect. Marcel is fully aware that he sometimes seems to be groping or stumbling on his way. Tilliette notes some of the colorful terms he uses to characterize his mode of philosophizing: exploration, drilling, reclamation, clearing away, dislocation, circumvallation, expedition, spelunking, circular prospecting. (*Pc* 10-11) Marcel admits that, in the last analysis, it is the will to explore that was always his fundamental disposition—in opposition perhaps to any kind of will to exploit.[9] Tilliette observes that this procedure clearly involves risks, indeed aporias, impasses, tunnels, wrong moves. It may be necessary to back track—but also, more often, he has luck: there are discoveries, unexpected perspectives, rich veins, encounters, and multiple connections, avenues of communication whose dense network attests the intellectual perspicacity of Gabriel Marcel. (*Pc* 10-11)

Tilliette also notes that the image of the way comes back repeatedly in Gabriel Marcel writings. His reflections follow the cadence of walking. His traveling thought knows what halting is but not stopping or resting, its does not construct a permanent shelter. The most vehement criticism it addresses to idealism is that of falsely immobilizing the mind, of lying about the itinerant nature of the human condition, for philosophy is a tireless search, an adventure, a personal

---

[9]Roger Troisfontaines, S.J., *De l'existence à l'être*, I (Paris: Vrin, 1953), 11. Translation mine. Henceforth cited as *Ex*.

itinerary. (*Pc* 42)   René Davignon likens Marcel's philosophy to creative investigation or a philosophy of "thinking thought" as opposed to systems of "thought thought." (*Mal* 159)

For Marcel this perpetual beginning again, which may seem scandalous to the scientist or the technician, is an inevitable part of all genuinely philosophical work. Perhaps it reflects in its own order the fresh start of every new awakening and of every birth. Does not the very structure of duration and of life show that philosophical thought is unfaithful to reality whenever it attempts to proceed from conclusion to conclusion towards a *Summa* which, in the end, needs only to be expounded and memorized paragraph by paragraph? The conviction that reality cannot be "summed up", that this is indeed the last way in which it can be apprehended, came to Marcel very early, partly as a result of reading Bradley. (*PE* 93) As Tilliette remarks, the refusal, at first provisional, then resolute, of systems and of systematic forms expresses, not an insufficient intellectual rigor, but a reasoned repulsion. (*Pc* 10-11)   Marcel himself characterizes his method as heuristic. (*Ex* 11)

The basic characteristic of existential philosophy, at least as Marcel conceived it, was to dispute the validity of the pretensions of totalizing thought. And it should be noted that he in no way believed in the possibility of a reconciliation between this thought and Marxism which he felt in its principles remains Hegelian or Hegelizing. (*St* 262) The moment we have a system, it seems we are concerned with exploiting it and managing it. And these verbs which apply so well to the material level lose something of their meaning, or at least their meaning is distorted, on the spiritual level. (*R* 252)

For a philosopher of existence, it is not a question, as it is for a classical philosopher, of beginning from a universal principle from which one would extract the consequences, but it is a question of concentrating first of all one's attention on a basic situation in which one participates but in relation to which one has enough distance. (*St* 262) As Jolin points out, in the "experiential thinking" Marcel advocates and represents, the most intense effort of attention must be directed to experience, but certainly this effort must not be squandered on what he would regard as the highly special, largely automatic, noetically neutral, and personally indifferent form of experience represented in pure sense data. The traditional empiricism Marcel rejects is especially that of Locke and Hume, in which the primary meaning of experience, the foundation of all knowing, is individual sense data. (*R* xxi) He also rejects the elaborate expressions in which philosophical language crystallizes itself, preferring the use of common everyday popular language because it deforms experience infinitely less. (*Mal* 158-59) Marcel corroborates Nussbaum's remarks about the Anglo-American tradition when he notes disapprovingly that students he met at Harvard during a visit to the United States, were dissuaded by their philosophy professors from seeking a relationship between the almost exclusively analytical thought in which they were being trained—and life, the problems that life poses to each one of us and which seemed in their eyes only to be the site of optional choices disengaged from any philosophical reference. (*St* 36)

Marcel, in contrast, grounds values in the concrete, in the life which we have to affirm, and he feels that that affirmation must not have a purely theoretical character. It must, on the contrary, be as much as possible specific to precise situations which experience consistently shows us to be of a tragic even anguished character. (*St* 167)

Tragic Wisdom

In "On the Ontological Mystery" Gabriel Marcel quotes Jacques Maritain as having said that there is nothing easier for a philosophy than to become tragic, it has only to let itself go to its human weight. Marcel disagrees with this opinion. He believes, instead, that the natural trend of philosophy leads it into a sphere where it seems that tragedy has simply vanished—evaporated at the touch of abstract thought. (*PE* 15) Abstraction makes it impossible not only to find a response to tragedy, to evil, to suffering and to death, but even to really consider or envisage them. (*Mal* 144) If we ignore the concrete, if we ignore the person, offering it up to some ideal truth, to some principle of pure inwardness, we become unable to grasp the tragic factors of human existence. We banish them, together with illness and everything akin to it, to some disreputable suburb of thought. (*PE* 15) The transcendent is denied, reduced to caricatural expressions which distort its essential character and the activity of verification is continually stressed. As a result, being is ignored—that inward realization of presence through love which infinitely transcends all possible verification because it exists in an immediacy beyond all conceivable mediation. (*PE* 5-6)

As Davignon notes, Marcel felt that it was his first and perhaps unique duty to make himself the defender of each of us against ourselves, against that extraordinary temptation of the inhuman to which—almost always without realizing it—so many succumb today. (*Mal* 156) What is tragic in the world of the soul, is that mortal dangers are not denounced there as they are sooner or later on the physical plane, by unmistakable symptoms, by suffering to which the organism is compelled to react. Here, unfortunately, the euphoria of the dying can be prolonged for generations, without the terminally ill, misled by blind clinicians, realizing that they are dying. The danger is that of degradation, perversion, foolishness in all the innumerable forms that it affects the human being, and whose diversity is like the counterweight or the countersign of our dignity and our eternal vocation. Faced with our situation Marcel is convinced that despair is possible in all its forms, at every instant, to all degrees. To despair is to let oneself go, to stop perpetually lifting oneself up. (*Mal* 65) He points out that one can despair of a person or of reality as a whole. This appears to be the result, or the immediate translation into other terms, of a kind of balance sheet. Inasmuch as we are able to evaluate the world of reality (and, when all is said and done, what we are unable to evaluate is for us as if it were not) we can find nothing in it which withstands that process of dissolution at the heart of things which we have discovered and traced. At the root of despair there is always this affirmation: There is nothing in the realm of reality to which we can give credit—no security, no guarantee. It is a statement of complete insolvency. (*PE* 15) Davignon points to Marcel's fierce denunciation of any attitude that would banish the possibility of falling into despair. Any philosophy that seeks to elude or side-step the themes of death, despair, and betrayal renders itself guilty of the worst betrayal imaginable, that of masking a menacing danger. (*Mal* 62-63)

He also does not hesitate to say that if a theology side-steps the tragic in any way whatsoever, if it substitutes for the reality of suffering and evil, what is only a fictitious image, an abstract effigy, giving itself to all kinds of logical manipulations, that theology gives to atheism a decisive reinforcement, since it is more than obvious that despite all the arguments that theologians and philosophers have used since the beginning, it is in the existence of evil and the suffering of innocents that atheism finds its permanent basis of supply. (*St* 248) Evil is real. We cannot deny its reality without threatening the fundamental seriousness of existence and this seriousness cannot be contested without existence degenerating into a non-sense or a kind of hideous buffoonery. (*St* 212) Evil is a mystery which for Marcel cannot be assimilated to the notion of something lacking, even to the sort of lack which is a deformity. (*Mass* 8) The triumph of evil, the triumph of death or despair are really the different modalities of a unique, very real, and redoubtable possibility. It is illusory to believe in any sort of reabsorption of evil in history, and it is no less so to have recourse to some dialectic artifice to integrate it into a superior synthesis. We find here, according to Marcel, one of the absolute limits of Hegelianism and its Marxist heirs. (*St* 208)

Marcel believes then that any thought that gives in to the complacences of optimism and refuses to make a place for the temptation to despair, dangerously ignores a fundamental given of our situation.   Philosophical atheism pretends to be animated by a will that is positive and Promethean, yet it ignores the temptation to despair which resides at the very center of our condition.   Marcel is convinced that consideration of this danger can open the way, perhaps not to a solution, but at least to an infinitely more precise formulation of the vital questions around which thought should move. (*St* 205)

Living clearly entails a risk: our being is to be realized, to be perfected. For Marcel, the "soul" is what is at stake. Incarnated in the time of history, it is during our existence, in the test of living, that we must unceasingly create our being, save our "soul." This test can be misunderstood or refused. At the limit, loss on the plane of being is strictly speaking perdition. If there is no life without risk, if life cannot be separated from a certain danger, it is in the essence of the soul to be able to be saved or lost, precisely to the degree that there is risk. The meaning of life is here. There is no other way of interpreting the human test. If the human test refers to the difficulties of existence and to the way in which we each react to grappling with them, it is in confronting them that we reveal the quality of our being, the seriousness of our commitment, and the authenticity of our person. We are always faced with the temptation to deny, to withdraw, and to harden ourselves. (*Mal* 59-60) Infinite, alas, are the resources despair disposes of to hide the paths through which regenerating assurances can reach us. (*St* 205) We can actively increase the amount of non-sense in the world. (*Mal* 98) The irreparable is clearly at the heart of becoming. With the passage of time we can become strangers to ourselves and lose understanding concerning ourselves. There is always a possibility of forgetfulness and betrayal of oneself.[10]

Marcel concludes that before the mystery of evil the only path that remains open is that of paradox, in the Kierkegaardian sense, that of a double affirmation which must be maintained in tension: Evil is real, and yet, evil is not real speaking in absolute terms. We must attain not a certitude, but faith in the possibility that it can be surmounted, certainly not abstractly, that is to say by adhering to a theory or a theodicy, but *hic et nunc. (St* 212)

There remains, however, a fundamental insecurity which must constantly stay present to our consciousness, this presence conferring to wisdom its authentic tragic character. *(St* 295) To aspire to wisdom is to aspire to make oneself in a certain way master of this situation. This is the mastery discussed in Chapter 1. Marcel points out that we know already that this mastery is undermined from within by forces which seem to coalesce to prevent its possibility—the very fact that, by the sentence which hangs over it, life carries death in it. *(St* 300-01) Wisdom then presents itself less as a state than as a goal. As a result, the spiritual equilibrium to be attained can in no way have a static character. It presents itself rather as a victory, let us not say over insecurity itself, but over the anguish which seems to be its inevitable consequence. *(PE* 37) Jolin remarks that the wisdom that refuses to abandon its home in the inexhaustibility of concrete experience is inevitably an unfinished and to that extent agonizingly insecure wisdom—a tragic wisdom. *(R* xxix)

Marcel also calls to our attention the mysterious proportion which seems to exist between the growth of fundamental insecurity and the growth of technology developed to protect us against the risks that threaten us (our health, our possessions, etc.) We have not ceased to believe in technology; that is, to envisage reality as a complex of problems. *(PE* 18) Marcel points out that there is no

---

[10]Gabriel Marcel, *Regards sur le théâtre de Paul Claudel* (Paris: Beauchesne, 1964), 37. Henceforth cited as *Reg.*

technical process which is not either actually or potentially at the service of some human desire or fear. All technology exists in relation to us, in so far as we are moved by desire or fear. (*Mass* 89) Yet, he correctly observes that the failure of technology *as a whole* is as discernible to us as its partial triumphs. To the question: what can humanity achieve? we continue to reply: We can achieve as much as our technology; but we are obliged to admit that technology is unable *to save men and women themselves*. It is even apt to conclude the most sinister alliance with the enemy we bear within us. (*PE* 18)

Marcel also observes that the more the disproportion grows between the claims of technical intelligence on the one hand, and the persisting fragility and precariousness of what remains its material substratum on the other, the more acute becomes the constant danger of despair which threatens this intelligence. From this standpoint there is truly an intimate dialectical correlation between the optimism of technical progress and the philosophy of despair which seems inevitably to emerge from it. (*PE* 19)

Marcel reacts strongly against the classical idea of the eminent value of *autarkia*, of one's own self-sufficiency. The perfect is not that which suffices for itself, or at least that perfection is that of a system, not of a being. If we deny our nature as created beings, we end up by claiming for ourselves attributes which are a sort of caricature of those that belong to the Uncreated. This parody, this pretended human autarky that we usurp for ourselves, inevitably degenerates into a resentment turned back on the very self for which such absurd claims are made. And that resentment flows out into the techniques of degradation. (*Mass* 75)

In the long run, all that is not done through Love and for Love must invariably end by being done against Love. Our condition manifests itself above all, however, in a tenacious resistance to life and to light, a resistance that is exercised to the profit of facility in all its forms. (*Reg* 37)

In discussing the dangers of technology, Marcel asks if a certain lived atheism is not more to be found in countries like ours than in communist countries regardless of what the statistics say which are more deceiving in this domain than in any other. This atheism has as its base satisfaction and numbness in the midst of a world more and more given over to technology which winds up functioning on its own. He wonders how it is possible not to see that this numbness leads to real spiritual death. (*St* 241) This lived atheism is characterized by a mitigated pragmatism, biosociological in character, based on a psychology and an ethics of conditioning. All disquiet and, more so, all anguish will be considered in this perspective as a sign of a psychosomatic disorder and one will count on a certain number of techniques to remedy this disturbance. (*St* 245) There is a permanent temptation for human intelligence, at least in this technological world to identify evil with a malfunctioning. A certain psychoanalysis will irresistibly tend to interpret what might be called—very improperly according to it—evil or sin as a maladjustment produced by a problem or a trauma. (*St* 205)

Davignon remarks that for Marcel, infidelity and unavailability are similar to despair and pessimism, they grow from the same roots. In each case one will treat life and one's being as a 'having' which leads to ontological emptiness, anguish, and even suicide. (*Mal* 72-73) Being unavailable, we know, is being centered on oneself, preoccupied with oneself in an excessive manner. It is as though at bottom each of us secreted a shell which becomes harder and harder and which imprisons us. (*Mal* 82)

In contrast, the soul which is at the disposal of others is consecrated and inwardly dedicated; it is protected against suicide and despair because it knows that it is not its own, and that the most legitimate use it can make of its freedom is precisely to recognize that it does not belong to itself; this recognition is the starting point of its activity and creativeness. (*PE* 28)

As we have seen, Marcel calls openness to the other intersubjectivity. It seems that there must be a reciprocity, an awakening. Only a relationship between one being and another can be called spiritual. What counts is the spiritual commerce between beings and it is not about respect but love. Intersubjectivity is perpetually threatened, however, because at every moment the self may close itself again and become a prisoner of itself, no longer considering the other except in relation to itself. But the possibility of opening to others (that is, in a completely different language, charity) is clearly one of the key certitudes to which Marcel came. It is on the level of agape, on the level of charity or intersubjectivity, that experience undergoes a certain transformation and takes on the value of a test. (*R* 254) We all must radiate light for the benefit of each other, while remembering that our role consists above all and perhaps exclusively in not presenting any obstacle to its passage through us. This, in spite of all appearances to the contrary, is an active role. It is an active role just because the self is a pretender, and a pretender whose duty it is to transcend or to destroy its own false claims. This can only be achieved through freedom and in a sense this is freedom. (*Mass* 263)

For Marcel, authentic human existence is existence-in-communion; it is you who gives me to myself. (*Edu* 40-41) I hope in you for us. (*R* 255) We are, not by nature, but by vocation, to be decentered or polycentered. (*St* 309) Happiness is from the other, and so he is ever mindful of the tenuous and fugitive nature of this communion. It is not something achieved once and for all, but rather a standing challenge. As Gallagher notes, the tragedy of human life is that the mode of existence which is its depth and fulfillment, is ceaselessly threatened.[11]

In assessing Marcel's work, Paul Ricoeur remarks on what he calls a hidden fissure which divides his thought. On the one hand there is an alarmed diagnosis of the signs of the times, and on the other a reflective celebration of incarnation, of concrete being. In his philosophy as a whole he is an antidualist, and yet there are two tonalities, one bitter, the other reassured, even joyous. As he very aptly puts it, in Marcel's work a metaphysics of light and a sociology of shadows confront each other incessantly. (*R* 252) The labyrinth of existence is crossed by rays of hope (*R* 255), authentic hope, which cannot be confused with an evasion of our particular situations. As Davignon observes, far from denying or fleeing the human condition,

---

[11]Kenneth T. Gallagher, *The Philosophy of Gabriel Marcel* (New York: Fordham University Press, 1962), 98. Cited in *Edu* 41. Henceforth cited as *PGM*.

hope plunges into the heart of reality to discover what withstands. (*Mal* 69)

Lévinas tells us that it was Marcel who first sensed positive modalities of thought, new meanings in this broken world, in this present dissolution. In the midst of the ruins, he says, Gabriel Marcel had already thought this ending and the beginnings it contains. He was witness to the end and initiator of the beginnings. Lévinas sees in Marcel a new wisdom, a new rationality beginning, a new notion of spirit. His thought is not mystical. Mysticism is still faithful to the order established by logic and to the absolute as being; it is correlative to logic. His is a fidelity to ontology despite the audacity of reaching the absolute without the work of concepts. Thus appears the end of a rationality attached exclusively, in words, to being. Modern philosophical literature prefers to play with verbal signs rather than take seriously the system that is inscribed in their utterance.

Being is not consciousness of self, it is, as we have seen, relationship with the other than oneself and awakening. For Lévinas, it is beneath the spirituality of the I awakened by the Thou in Marcel, who is in agreement with Buber, that new meaning lies. The spirit is not the Said, it is the Saying that goes from the Same to the Other.[12]

It should also be noted that the correlation of hope and despair in Marcel subsists until the end. The two seem to be inseparable. The world we live in permits —and may even seem to counsel—absolute despair, yet it is only such a world that can give rise to an unconquerable hope—a hope springing from humility and not from pride, that is, a hope in what does not depend on ourselves, the only genuine hope. (*PE* 19) For this reason, he is thankful to the great pessimists in the history of thought for they carried through an inward experience which needed to be made. It is the radical possibility of this experience that no apologetics should disguise. (*PE* 16-17)

---

[12]Emmanuel Lévinas, *Entre nous* (Paris: Grasset, 1991), 73-74.

CHAPTER 6

DRAMATIC CREATION

Gabriel Marcel on Dramatic Creation

Let us begin now to explore the nature of dramatic creation in an effort to understand its fecundity, its relation to thought, and its connection to the transcendent. We will begin with Marcel's views and then analyze a text by Claudel on dramatic creation which will reveal interesting parallels with both Marcel and Martin Heidegger.

Gabriel Marcel relates that from his earliest childhood he witnessed in his family circle differences of temperament and opinion which prematurely forced him to become aware of the *insolubilia* involved in even the most simple relationships. He realized that there can exist incompatible outlooks and divergent opinions which a truthful and fair mind can never really reconcile. This led him to perceive that there is a certain radical weakness in the faculty of judgment and to assume the existence of a domain beyond speech in which harmony can be discerned and in a sense even restored. It was music that offered him an irrefutable example of a kind of supra-rational unity and he believed it was drama that was to establish and to promote this unity. From his earliest years, Marcel was also haunted by the theatre. He tells us that as a child imaginary characters replaced for him the brothers and sisters that he so cruelly missed in real life.(*PE* 78)

Marcel warns that whoever approaches his work will have to conceive his philosophy in terms of his drama and his drama in terms of music. (*PE* 80) Just as the appearance of the existential in the theatre notably preceded the publication of philosophical existential works, and even the rediscovery of Kierkegaard,[1] Marcel's drama illustrated and confirmed in advance all that he was later to write on the purely philosophical plane concerning knowledge in its capacity to transcend objectivity (*PE* 78)

Dramatic work, for Marcel, was also the way out of the labyrinth into which he had been led by his abstract thinking; through it he hoped to emerge into the light of an organized human landscape whose structure he wanted to understand. Nevertheless, the pattern of this landscape was not really different from that of his own subterranean regions, in which his thought struggled to understand itself and to ensure its grasp on a reality which continually eluded it. (*PE* 80) It might then be said, as Ricoeur does, that his plays served to get rid of phantoms, to exorcize them, preparing the way for what the philosopher was not yet able to say. (*R* 232) His dramatic vision, what he saw with the help of his characters, was an anticipation of what could appear to him only later at the philosophical level. (*R* 234)

Marcel was convinced that it is in drama and through drama that metaphysical thought grasps and defines itself *in concreto*. (*PE* 15) The dramatic character is like an embodied philosophical example. It is precisely because it enjoys a kind of autonomy that it can be so stimulating philosophically. (*R* 236) When reflecting on the central problems of moral philosophy, Marcel would always invite his students to do something that they were not accustomed to doing. He asked them to dramatize. He would invite them to imagine someone grappling with the problem under discussion. He would then advise them to put themselves in the place of that person. The same advice he felt would be good for preachers. He was convinced that reflection cannot function where imagination is lacking and that there is no charity, no *agape* worthy of the name without imagination. Clearly imagination

---

[1]Gabriel Marcel, *Théâtre et religion* (Lyon: Editions Emmanuel Vitte, 1958), 68. Henceforth cited as *Tr*.

cannot suffice in concrete situations; it must be surpassed, yet not abandoned, for it must always remain intimately present to the thought of the one who seeks. (*St* 194-95)

Marcel aimed at a restoration of that unity of poetic vision and philosophic creativity of which the great pre-Socratic philosophers offer us one of the first known examples. (*Mass* 39) As Ricoeur remarks, everything in his work comes from drama and everything leads to it as well, especially the analysis of those experiences he calls "ontological," insofar as these experiences have a dramatic character. (*R* 230) Marcel felt that theory, or even discourse as such, always threatens intersubjectivity because beings are treated in the third person. In drama, the subject transcends objectivization, since he is treated as a first person, and the other becomes for him a You. (*St* 271)

When we understand that the connection between philosophy and drama in Marcel's case was the closest, the most intimate possible, we can comprehend why he claims that his philosophy is existential to the degree that it is simultaneously drama, that is, dramatic creation. It is precisely because he believed that the subject can be adequately thought only where it is allowed to speak for itself, otherwise, as we have said, it is inevitably objectified and consequently distorted. (*R* 230) And so we see that the difficulties raised by the elaboration of a philosophy of existence come from the fact that such a philosophy risks at every moment to falsify the existence to which it refers and to change it into something else which in a certain way denies it. Dramatic expression is, on the other hand, existential by its nature because the characters there are treated as subjects who eventually decide for themselves. It might be said that it is in drama that thought actualizes itself, it becomes manifest, not only for the public, *but for itself*. It is completely natural then that the existentialist philosopher become a playwright as both Sartre and Marcel did.

Drama was for Marcel a sort of prospecting that favored the blossoming of philosophic reflection. The theater also played the role of partial challenge to what is too schematic in philosophy. (*Mal* 149)

As one might expect, however, Marcel hated didactic plays in which fundamental questions are only raised on the level of discussion and not on the level of existence. (*Mal* 155) In these plays questions are debated and theses clash. In other words problems are seen from the outside. Nothing is really lived and that is why, according to him, these works have not survived. (*Reg* 13) This is, of course, not to imply that playwrights should avoid the disputes which appear in our world. On the contrary, they must instead make these conflicts theirs so that through them and through their work these disputes can be overcome—musically, however, rather than logically or dialectically. (*Tr* 95) Conflict is resolved in harmony—a harmony in which there is nothing that resembles a logical reconciliation or a dialectical synthesis. (*Tr* 92) Such a harmony can only be realized at the dramatic level and cannot bear the least resemblance to what Marcel calls the miserable intellectual compromises that a certain progressivism tries to achieve between ideas that exclude one another. (*Tr* 93)

The theatre did not attract Marcel as spectacle either, but rather as a privileged form of expression that conceals itself, as it were, behind the subjects whom it confronts. (*PE* 78) According to him the most profound discovery of Schopenhauer, the one by which in a certain way, despite his residual Platonism, he anticipates the philosophers of existence, is perhaps the discovery of the intrinsic insufficiency of representation, of the spectacle. (*St* 86) Marcel's own plays are interior dramas devoid of spectacle, for he insists that mystery is not spectacle, but rather a metaphysical opening. (*Edu* 52)

Thus, for Marcel, the authentic dramatic work is not destined to spectators as mere spectators; it must not simply be a visual pleasure. It interests the human being behind the spectator, the human being engaged in the dangerous pilgrimage of life. It is necessary that the human being, the *homo viator*, recognize in the dramatic action unfolding before him something that concerns him essentially or vitally, something in which he feels himself implicated. (*Tr* 75) The dramatist is to lead the spectator to the focal point in himself where his thoughts can proliferate, not on the abstract level, but on the level of action, and enfold all the characters of a play without any decrease in their reality or in their irreducible individuality.[2]

The chief function of the theatre is then not to relate the particular to the general or to a law or to an idea, but to awaken or re-awaken in us the consciousness of the infinite which is concealed in the particular. To Marcel's mind, in this way alone can the dramatist penetrate to our center and arrive at that zone of concrete universality which music and metaphysics reach by other convergent ways. (*3P* 27)

In drama, much more so than in other art forms, the artist must be capable of sacrifice. He must forget himself in favor of the being which he has created and whose liberty he must defend; he must literally place himself at the service of a certain truth which is immanent to the beings and the relations that bind them. It is this that forbids him from using them for a purpose that would be his own in so far as he is a moralist or a politician disguised as a dramatic author. (*Tr* 78)

Marcel was convinced that humility is at the source of everything that is authentically and durably great. (*Tr* 87) The dramatic author must consider himself simply as the site or place where a certain truth must appear and he must be sufficiently detached from himself to effectively become that site. This is the meaning of the humility whose necessity Marcel proclaimed. (*Tr* 94-95) It is an act of transcendence or of renunciation effectuated by what one usually calls the creative imagination. (*Mal* 149)

Concerning his own plays, Marcel was utterly convinced that they were not invented but on the contrary had been given to him, and even imposed upon him. Under those conditions, his limited but quite delicate task was to penetrate, by a fraternal impulse, into the interior life of others in order to become for them, so to speak, *helpful from within*, rather than from without. (*PGM* xv)·

As Marcel looked back on his work in later years what struck him was that he still found in his plays a kind of living interest or freshness that seemed to be

---

[2]Gabriel Marcel, "The Drama of the Soul in Exile," in *Three Plays* (London: Secker & Warburg, 1952), 21. Henceforth cited as *3P*.

somewhat lacking in his philosophical writings which were in some way too explicit, too summary. Drama, he concludes, is like living tissue; it is more capable of internal regeneration than is properly philosophical thinking. (*R* 236) In another context he said that his plays might be compared to an underground stream whose overflow, often scarcely perceptible, irrigated, as it were, his speculative thought.[3]

On yet another occasion, Marcel compared his work as a whole to a country like Greece, which comprises at the same time a continental part and islands. The continental part is his philosophical writing. The islands are his plays. Why this comparison? Because just as it is necessary to make a crossing to get to an island, so it is necessary to leave the shore behind to get to his dramatic work, to dramatic creation. The element which unites the continent and the islands in Marcel's work is music. The priority belongs to music. Music is truly the deepest level. The reflecting subject must then in some way leave himself behind, forget himself in order to yield completely and be absorbed in the beings he has conceived and whom he must try to bring to life. (*R* 230-31) This is precisely the alienation of self so painfully depicted in Claudel's ode analyzed in Chapter 2. This is the abandonment most resisted by our impulse for mastery and control.

The playwright is an artist who creates living persons. However, if these persons are mere mouthpieces or marionettes, then there is no creation. As we have said, the playwright must allow these persons independence, and to do so he must submerge himself. There is then no authentic dramatic creation without this alienation of self which the playwright effects in favor of the beings to whom he has given life.[4] Marcel likens this process to God's creation of humanity in His image, but truly independent of Him. The spirituality of the theatre is above all the power of incarnation. (*Tr* 55)

---

[3]Gabriel Marcel, *The Existential Background of Human Dignity* (Cambridge, MA: Harvard University Press, 1963), 5.

[4]Gabriel Marcel, "Influence du Théâtre," *Revue des Jeunes* (5 March 1935): 355. Henceforth cited as *IT*.

If the playwright has been successful in his creation, his work will provoke in those who see and hear it a communion and an active participation in the play with the creator. The spectator will be freed from the systems that normally imprison him in a certain way of seeing and judging. He will in a sense escape from his mortal condition: for a time he will breathe existence in a more ample fashion. He will commune not only with what happens on stage, but beyond that particular limited action, with the infinite number of tragedies which he suddenly realizes his brothers endure. But it is not only his sense of reality which is deepened and sharpened, a breach will also be opened in that opaque armor which protects us and weighs us down—a breach through which perhaps a new breath might penetrate—the breath of the Spirit. (*IT* 361-62)

The mediators of the union of playwright and spectator are the actors. Like the playwright and the spectators, they are called upon to empty themselves in order to become the roles created by the playwright. In a sense they are both spectator and creator. They must study the part and then through their own bodies make the creation of the playwright perceptible. They are the representation or reification of a presence. They bring about the mysterious union of the creator and the spectator, by a second creation, which manifests the infinite power, and incredible fecundity of the Spirit. (*Edu* 52-53) In art, subjectivity tends to pass over into an intersubjectivity which is entirely different from the objectivity science honors so much. It completely surpasses the limits of the individual consciousness taken in isolation. (*R* xxviii)

Moran notes that in creation, the act of the poet is neither autonomous nor heteronomous. A true work of art is more than the poet's act; it "testifies" to a gift of transcendence. Yet the reception of the inspiration is itself an act of the poet. It is impossible to break down the creative event into distinct elements, one contributed by the poet and one by being or transcendence. The work is entirely the poet's and entirely a gift. Marcel says that it is a response to an invocation. (*Edu* 29) When writing of the great 19th century poet Rilke, Marcel notes that what Rilke teaches us better than anyone is that there exists a receptivity which is really creation itself under another name. He concludes that the most genuinely receptive being is at the same time the most essentially creative. (*Edu* 28) In this same context, Gallagher cites Heidegger's essay "Hölderlin and the Essence of Poetry," in which he speaks of the poet as one who intercepts divine signs: "This intercepting is an act of receiving and yet at the same time a fresh act of giving." (*PGM* 169)

Marcel also speaks of a humble withdrawal which befits recollection and whereby we renew our contact with the ontological basis of our being. (*PE* 20-21) Such a withdrawal in recollection is a presupposition of aesthetic creativity itself. Artistic creation, like scientific research, excludes the act of self-centering and self-hypnotism which is, ontologically speaking, pure negation. (*PE* 20-21)

True artists—in paint, or stone, or music, or words—experience a relationship to the transcendent in the most authentic and profound way. That is, of course, if they do not yield to the innumerable temptations to which artists are exposed today: the temptation to startle, to innovate at all costs, to shut oneself up in a private world leaving as few channels as possible open for communication with the world, and so on. (*Mass* 23)

It is presence, Marcel tells us, whose virtue is a mysterious incitement to create (*PE* 22), and we think of that female presence that tormented Claudel: the muse who is Grace. Marcel assures us that a presence is a reality; it is a kind of influx; it depends upon us to be permeable to this influx, but not, to tell the truth, to call it forth. We are to maintain ourselves actively in a permeable state. There is a mysterious interchange between this free act and the gift granted in response to it. (*PE* 24) The ultimate significance of creation is its deep-rootedness in being. (*PE* 20-21)

Where there is creation, then, there can be no degradation, and to the extent that technology is creative, or implies creativity, it is not degrading in any way. (*PE* 20) After all, the error of empiricism consists only in ignoring the part of invention and creative initiative involved in any genuine experience. It might also be said that its error is to take experience for granted and to ignore its mystery. (*PE* 96)

In his preface to Gallagher, Marcel says he is in complete agreement with him when he affirms that as soon as there is creation, in whatever degree, we are in the realm of being. But Marcel points out that the converse is equally true: that is to say, there is doubtless no sense in using the word "being" except where creation, in some form or other, is in view. (*PGM* xiii)

We can now understand why he remarks that his inquiry into being presupposes an affirmation in regard to which he is, in a sense, passive, and of which he is the stage rather than the subject. (*PE* 8) This inquiry into being has clearly been side-stepped today, except of course by Heidegger and his followers. For Marcel, however, it is crucial to know if wisdom, when it is something other that a collection of utilitarian formulas which are in the final analysis technical, can take root in any other ground than that from which poetry originates and from which it draws its nourishment. (*St* 303) Is it not one of the duties of the philosopher, or more precisely of the philosopher-poet, to endeavor to snatch, as it were, the very soul of an event? (*Mass* 41)

Marcel insists that reason should not defend itself against gifts whose source it does not know and refuse them as one might refuse contraband merchandise. Reason, though it recognizes itself as overwhelmed by the music of Bach, expands itself, on the contrary, to welcome that light; for, in its depths, reason has a presentiment, though a very indistinct one, that this light is of the same nature as reason itself. Reason should make it a point of honor to proclaim this identity, to whose origin and nature nevertheless it has no clue. (*Mass* 253)

Paul Claudel on Dramatic Creation

It is in his essay "La Poésie est un art " ("Poetry Is an Art ") that Claudel makes his perhaps most important statement on the nature of theatre and dramatic creation. He begins by telling us that with drama, as opposed to epic poetry or the novel, we penetrate the most obscure region of the human mind—the region of dreams. These are the subterranean regions to which Marcel refers. Claudel tells us that in our dreams, our mind, having been reduced to a passive or semi-passive state, becomes a stage invaded by phantoms who seduce us into a collaboration which will result in an event. Claudel calls drama "a directed dream." (*Oc* XVIII, 17) The theme is imposed, he tells us, and we recall that Marcel said as much. Then characters emerge recruited by a masked impresario. Slowly but surely everything falls into place. Claudel explains that it is not like in real theaters, those in which one pays for one's seat, where only inarticulated communication is attempted between the audience and the stage. Here, between the two there is an organic supplication like that between the embryo and mother. The initiative comes from the stage, but the audience, what a chorus it becomes! He also speaks of two directors, one on the right and another on the left, who explain to the actors what they are to do. He speaks, too, of the mounting enthusiasm and of the action which creates its own law and its own verisimilitude. "Words literally gush up from under our feet!" The audience is in tears and demands a conclusion "with the avidity of a vortex." Finally, Claudel exclaims: "Ah! just one voice was not enough for the poet, he needed this group working together on stage. This sort of sacrifice, this type of demand, of seizing, this invisible aspiration to which the dramatist does nothing more than respond was needed by a multitude famished for absolutes hidden behind daily illusions, famished for truth on this elevated stage . . . but why only the dramatist? Not only the dramatist, the poet, all poets whoever they may be . . . aspiration, inspiration." (*Oc*, XVIII, 18)

We are reminded here that Marcel, too, spoke of sacrifice, of   the transcendent, and of the poet as one who responds. But also of interest is the presence of a masked impresario and the mention of embryo and mother in connection with the creative experience. Then there is also the topography of Claudel's dream scape.

Let us first consider the presence of the masked impresario. Heidegger's remarks concerning concealment in *The Origin of the Work of Art* are of interest in this regard. Concealment, we learn, can be a refusal or merely a dissembling. We are never fully certain whether it is one or the other. Concealment conceals and dissembles itself. The open space in the midst of beings, the clearing, is never a rigid stage with a permanently raised curtain on which the play of being runs its course. Rather, the clearing happens only as a double concealment. According to Heidegger, this double concealment—in the form of either refusal or dissembling—belongs to the nature of truth. This, however, does not imply that truth, which he calls unconcealedness, is at bottom falsehood. Nor does it mean that truth is never itself, but rather that truth is always also its opposite. The concealing denial denotes the opposition in the nature of truth. Heidegger calls it the opposition of the primal conflict.[5]

We hear curious echoes of this in both Marcel and Claudel. We saw that for Marcel mystery is not spectacle but rather a metaphysical opening. He, too, spoke of the interior stage. And we hear Claudel ask: "But what is one to do? Admit that all agreement is the result not only of a geometry, but of a struggle, and that truth is composed of tendencies in opposite directions. . . . It is this idea of truths that meet not in a static equilibrium, but in an effort around a common point and on divergent points, that is the crux of my entire intellectual enterprise." (*Oc*, XX, 428) Maurice Blanchot attests to this when he says of Claudel: "What strikes one about him is the essential discordance, the powerful clash, contained, ill-contained, of movements without harmony, a formidable mix of contrary needs, opposed exigencies,

---

[5]Martin Heidegger, *Poetry, Language, Thought*, trans. by Albert Hofstadter (New York: Harper & Row, 1971), 53-55. This source is henceforth cited as *PLT*.

unmatched qualities and irreconcilable aptitudes."[6] And here we recall Marcel's exigence of harmony, of rising to another plane on which conflicts can be resolved musically.

When describing the concealment which is dissembling, Heidegger speaks of one being placing itself in front of another being, the one helping to hide the other. A being appears, but it presents itself as other than it is. (*PLT*, 54)   In Claudel's dream we have penetrated the concealment of "daily illusion," yet concealment is indeed double, for we still have a masked impresario and actors who reveal truth by dissembling. We should undoubtedly note, too, in this connection, that for Claudel dissemblance is somehow a feminine attribute. "Woman never comes out, is only completely herself as an actress."[7]

The feminine, however, is also present in other dimensions. The dramatic creation itself was called an embryo and the inner theatre a womb. The dream which occasions this creative activity is somehow also connected with the feminine. "The man who sleeps with a sigh takes another bite in the profound earth. All is silent, for it is the hour when the earth gives drink and none of her children has stopped at her liberal breast in vain; poor and rich, the child and the old man, the just and the guilty, the judge with the prisoner, and man as the animals, all together, like little brothers drink! All is mystery, for here is the hour when man communicates with his mother. The sleeper sleeps and cannot awaken, he has the nipple and will not let go, this mouthful is also his." (*OC*, III, 51)

Dreams somehow connect man to the earth which, for Claudel, is feminine. Interestingly enough, just as Claudel associates the feminine with dissembling and concealment, Heidegger speaks of earth as the Closed that corresponds to concealment. The world is the Open that corresponds to clearing. World and earth

---

[6]Maurice Blanchot, *Le Livre à venir* (Paris: Gallimard, 1959), 85.

[7]Paul Claudel, *Journal*, I & II (Paris: Gallimard, 1968-69), I, 175. This source is henceforth cited as *J*, I or *J*, II.

are always intrinsically and essentially in conflict, the conflict of clearing and
concealing. (*PLT* 55)

This notion of conflict brings to mind Claudel's famous saying: "Without
opposition no composition." (*Th*, II, 1474) It will also lead us now to a discussion
of the topography of Claudel's dream world. We note first of all that there are two
directors in his dream—one on the left and one on the right. Inspiration, however,
comes from below. We saw that "words literally gush up from under our feet." The
audience, which is likened to a womb, contributes to the creative process by
demanding a conclusion "with the avidity of a vortex." The vertical dimension is
also suggested by "the elevated stage." We then discern both vertical and horizontal
dimensions. "From above and from below, from left to right, the different elements
unite to aspirate the actors and the drama." (*Th*, II, 1473)

With this we have touched a central figure of Claudelian thought. We will
begin our study of it by examining what the division between right and left means.
Most obvious is its allusion to the distinction between yes and no, good and evil, true
and false. (*OC*, V, 161) On another level it suggests the distinction between
masculine and feminine. The left hand maintains, sustains, prepares, proposes,
presents; the right hand works and operates. (*Opr* 1356) The left hand consolidates;
the right measures. (*J*, II, 769) The left conserves and nourishes; the right fashions
and molds. (*Oc*, XXV, 559) From the left come the resources to respond to the
demands of the right. (*Oc*, XXI, 422) The left supports the right. But it is with the
right that new things are acquired, it does and gives. The left receives, chooses, and
eliminates. (*Oc*, XIX, 273) The right hand holds lightening, the left strangles the
serpent. (*Op* 286) Claudel's Joan of Arc held a banner in her left hand and a sword
in her right. (*Oc*, XIV, 279) In *Jet de pierre* (*Stone's Throw*) we see "the left hand
out to conquer the right hand" (*Th*, II, 1245) and in *La Lune à la recherche d'elle-
même* (*The Moon In Search of Herself*) we hear: "Nothing like the left hand to
enchant, to fetter the right hand and to prevent it from doing damage." (*Th*, II, 1333)

It is when we add to this horizontal extension the vertical dimension present
in the dream as "vortex (or abyss)" and "that elevated stage" that the central figure

of Claudelian thought becomes clear: it is the cross. "Here is the sublime intersection in which heaven is joined to the earth by man. Here is the judgment between the right and the left, the separation of high and low. Here is the oblation and the sacrifice! Here is the most holy Middle, the center from which the four lines diverge, here is the ineffable point."[8] Here, indeed, is the sacrifice. Here too, however, we also encounter the central figure of Heideggerian thought—the fourfold. For Heidegger the ontological content of the world is differentiated by the fourfold which he names earth and sky, the mortal and the divine. The fourfold is the parameter indicating those sectors which in their mutual interplay constitute a totality essentially related to language and being.[9] As perhaps no other thing can, the cross would seem to gather to itself earth and heaven, the divine and the mortal as the simple oneness of the four Heidegger calls the fourfold.

Heidegger says that the world and things do not subsist alongside one another; they penetrate each other. Thus the two traverse a middle and in it, they are one; they are intimate. The middle of the two is intimacy. But this intimacy of the world and thing is not a fusion. Intimacy obtains only where the intimate—world and thing—divides itself cleanly and remains separated. In the midst of the two, in the between of world and thing, in their *inter*, division prevails: a *dif-ference*. (*PLT* 202)

We are reminded at almost every turn that Claudel's geometry is painful. As we have seen it both unites and separates. Heidegger says of pain that it rends, it tears asunder, it separates, yet at the same time it draws everything to itself, gathers it to itself. Its rending is a separating that gathers. It draws and joins together what is held apart in separation. Pain joins the rift of dif-ference; it is the dif-ference itself. (*PLT* 204) We are struck by the structural and functional similarities of this concept

---

[8]Paul Claudel, *Théâtre*, I (Paris: Gallimard, 1969), 844. Henceforth cited as *Th* I.

[9]David A. White, *Heidegger and the Language of Poetry* (Lincoln: University of Nebraska Press, 1978), 30.

in the work of both men.

We have noted how the topology of Claudel's dream scape contains vertical and horizontal dimensions which suggest the cross and therefore the notion of sacrifice. Yet, it might be said that the sacrifice which Claudel names is actually of another, although kindred, type. It is explained by the cry: "Words literally gush up from under our feet!" To gush (*jaillir*) suggests an outpouring or libation; or, as Heidegger notes, an authentic gift. The consecrated libation is what the word for strong outpouring, gush, really designates: gift and sacrifice. Heidegger tells us that in the gift of the outpouring the mortal and the divine each dwells in their different ways. Earth and sky dwell in the gift of the outpouring. In the gift of the outpouring earth and sky, mortal and divine dwell together all at once. They are enfolded into a single fourfold. (*PLT* 173)

This poured gift can of course be assimilated to the cross. For Claudel, however, there is more than a gushing libation; there is also the avidity of the vortex, a demand, a seizing, aspiration, inspiration. He tells us that the poet realizes that it is not about representation, but about dreaming. "But therein lies the surprising contradiction! from this magnetic ecstasy, from this fascinated silence, what emerges? a kind of religious furor, a savage need for madness, violence, howling, and frenzied coursing!" (*Th*, II, 1322)

For Claudel the artist is a dreamer and as such he is primarily characterized as the one who responds. Heidegger says that mortals speak insofar as they listen. This speaking that listens and accepts is responding. This responding is a hearing. It hears because it listens to the command of stillness (*PLT* 209-10), Claudel's "fascinated silence."

Heidegger refers to his exegetical essays on literary texts as illuminations and as Kevin Hart says, although his illuminations are in some sense answerable to their texts there is no method by which one can pass from text to illumination.[10] What

---

[10]Kevin Hart, *The Trespass of the Sign* (Cambridge: Cambridge University Press, 1989), 254.

could be closer to Claudel's "aspiration, inspiration" and to Marcel's receptivity?

CHAPTER 7

GABRIEL MARCEL READS PAUL CLAUDEL

In the conversations between Gabriel Marcel and Paul Ricoeur published in 1968, Ricoeur attempts to assess Gabriel Marcel's contributions to thought. He affirms that Marcel was the one who made the connection between the philosophy of sensation and that of existence, laying the foundation for what Merleau-Ponty and others later called the phenomenology of perception. Marcel, however, disputes this affirmation. He instead asserts that it was Paul Claudel who anticipated this connection in his poetic art; more precisely, in his theory of knowledge, in his idea of *co-naissance*. Although Ricoeur will insist that Marcel opened the way to a philosophy of the body-subject and gave philosophy the means of thinking embodiment by taking the body, rather than language, as the primary focus of his reflection on existence; he, too, acknowledges the importance of Claudel's contribution though he limits it to the domain of speech, of the word.

Marcel was always careful to credit his sources. He had a horror of ingratitude and amnesia and he believed that here he owed a specific debt to Claudel, even though Claudel was not a philosopher in the technical sense of the term. But in a person of genius, don't barriers and divisions break down, so that poetry and philosophy are joined? he asks. Marcel did not think he was being unfair to himself in pointing out what he owed to Claudel's theory and practice of poetry. (*R* 222) In discussing cognition, for instance, Marcel speaks of recognizing that knowledge is, as it were, environed by being, that it is interior to being in a certain sense. But then he is quick to acknowledge that this idea is analogous to the one Paul Claudel tried to define in his *Art*

111

poétique (Poetic Art). From this standpoint, contrary to what epistemology seeks vainly to establish, there exists well and truly a mystery of cognition; knowledge is contingent on a participation in being for which no epistemology can account because it continually presupposes it. *(Pe 8)*

Claudel's idea of *co-naissance* again comes to mind when Marcel meditates on the metaphysical value of the word *with*, so rarely recognized by philosophers, which corresponds neither to a relationship of inherence or immanence, nor to a relationship of exteriority. He speaks of genuine *coesse*, that is to say, genuine intimacy. *(Pe 25)* Claudel's idea undoubtedly also underlies Marcel's *reconnaissance*—the act of recognizing others which is so intimately tied to intersubjectivity. *(R 245)*

But there is more. Ricoeur detects a Claudelian strain in Marcel's philosophy of freedom which stresses the freedom of response. He contrasts it to Jaspers' philosophy of freedom which emphasizes choice so much, self-choice in anxiety. For Marcel the freedom of response goes beyond the freedom of choice, and anxiety is not the central theme of what he would call his philosophy of existence. He also differs greatly from Heidegger in this regard. In fact, it became more and more clear to him—and here he acknowledges Claudel's influence once again—that there could be an existential experience of joy and of fullness. *(R 241-42)*

When discussing the importance of music, he also brings Claudel to mind. Here he insists upon the importance of not identifying reason with understanding. In his spiritual economy, understanding fills an indispensable but subordinate office: that of the calculable. Certainly this calculating understanding finds plenty of work to do, he tells us, but it is by definition impossible for it to explain anything or to plumb the depths of anything. To illustrate his point he turns to some lines from Claudel's *La Ville* (*The City*). The engineer Besme speaks to the poet Coeuvre:

> Make clear to me whence comes this breath by your mouth transformed
> into words.
> For, when you speak, like a tree that with all its leaves
> Stirs in the silence of Noon, within our hearts peace imperceptibly
> succeeds to thought.

By means of this song without music and this word that has no voice,
we are put in accord with the melody of the world.

You explain nothing, o poet, but all things become comprehensible
through you. (*Th*, I, 428)[1]

Although he understood that these lines referred to the lyric poet, in spite of that, Marcel was convinced they still retained their meaning for someone like him, for whom the union of philosophy and music was so profound. (*PGM* xv)

For Marcel, Claudel was one of the most complete and, in some ways, the most disconcerting artistic personalities that has ever existed. (*Reg* 42) His was a marvelous intelligence, according to Marcel; an intelligence which he characterizes as lyrical. It never exhausted itself. It was somehow a sacred office, a participation in the mystery which makes things be and know each other. (*Reg* 46)

We have already noted that Marcel sought a restoration of the unity of poetic vision and philosophic creativity of which the great pre-Socratic philosophers offer us one of the first known examples. It is then not a matter of mere chance that he was able to appreciate the sudden lightning-flashes of penetration into human reality found in the works of a writer like Claudel but which the specialist philosopher today seems condemned to miss: exactly as one misses a promotion, or a train. (*Mass* 39-40)

Just as Lacan discovered the Oedipal dimension in Claudel and touted this as a confirmation of Freud's theories, Marcel notes that the appearance of the existential in Claudel notably preceded the publication of philosophical existential works, and even the rediscovery of Kierkegaard. The poetic surge of the existential is clearly discernable in Claudel's first theatrical works. (*Tr* 68)

Marcel claims that this century has witnessed a prodigious enlargement of the theatrical field. It might be said, in fact, that a new dimension has emerged. In this development he is convinced that Paul Claudel must be given not only an eminent, but a central place. (*Tr* 14-15) He asserts that the dramatic work of Paul Claudel represented a revolution without analogue in France. (*Reg* 13) It is in opposition to the

---

[1]Cited in *St* 239-40.

whole French dramatic tradition. Neither psychological, nor social or critical, Marcel characterizes it instead as cosmic or ontological—a theatre in which something essential is always at stake. He feared, however, that people were incapable not only of appreciating, but even of understanding the extraordinary grandeur of Claudel's work. He thought Claudel's form, in particular, was difficult to assimilate for people who have not received an adequate formation. (*Tr* 17-18)

According to Marcel, it is with *The City* that one must start if one wants to try to define the Claudelian contribution to the theater, for he believed it to be the matrix for all of Claudel's later work. (*Tr* 22) Claudel tells us that he wrote the play during his conversion. The city represented for him a sort of Sodom and Gomorrah in which he found himself plunged and from which he had to escape at any cost. It was a stifling world, a world in which people expanded as much as possible and left absolutely no space. There was no air. People were squeezed together. There was no feeling, or charity, or patience but a sort of mutual bad-temper and continual tension, a secret war of everyone against everyone. There was a kind of mistrust, hatred, and terror which reigned all at once in the way the different classes related to one another.[2] Claudel had not yet completely left Sodom and Gomorrah nor been completely integrated into the city of God when he wrote *The City*. Marcel contends that what gives this play its grandeur is precisely the fact that the author is in some way divided between his characters. Claudel himself admits, regarding the curious character of Avare—the anarchist, that he found in anarchy an almost instinctive reaction against that suffocating world. The anarchists were like drowning men who were gasping for air. (*Tr* 21-22) For Marcel then, one of the things that gives *The City* its richness and its depth is that anarchy finds its mouthpiece in Avare, and that the voice which announces and exalts the destruction of the established order is a part of what must be called the Claudelian interior orchestra. (*Reg* 28)

Let us recall Marcel's fierce denunciation of any attitude that would banish the possibility of falling into despair or that would side-step the tragic or the reality of

---

[2]Paul Claudel, *Mémoires improvisées* (Paris: Gallimard, 1969). Cited in *Tr* 20-21.

suffering and evil. And so we understand the great importance Marcel gives to the words of Besme in *The City*, which seem to translate with an unsurpassed expressive force what nihilism can be for a man of this time. He cites them frequently in his works. As Davignon points out, they illustrate the aspiration of man not *towards*, but *by* death, which is at the heart of pessimism and at the origin of the despair and nihilism which Marcel felt are always menacing. (*Mal* 115)

> Besme: The pain of death, the knowledge of death.
>
> It was while I was working, in peace lining up numbers on the paper,
>
> That that thought for the first time filled me like a dark flash:
>
> Now I do this, and soon I will do some other thing;
>
> Soon I will *be* gay, or I will *be* sad; good, bad, greedy, generous, patient, irritable;
>
> And I *am* living, until I will *be* no more.
>
> But as each of those adjectives rests on that permanent word, in what way do I myself continue? (*Th*, I, 431)

And a little further on:

> Besme: Nothing is...
>
> Listen! I will repeat those words which I have said: nothing is.
>
> I have seen and I have touched
>
> The horror of uselessness, adding to what is not the proof of my hands.
>
> Nothingness does not need to proclaim itself by a mouth that can say: I am.
>
> Here is my prey and such is the discovery that I have made. (Th, I, 441)

Nihilism is presented here as a fact arrived at by the wise man who has seen everything dissipate or rather reduce itself to a vain accounting. (*St* 239-40)

For Marcel, what is proposed to us in *The City* is a global and tragic consciousness of the modern world symbolized by the great modern city where individuals are lost in an anonymous unity; they are conscious of being lost there and are therefore engaged in a confrontation with death with no way out. (*Reg* 24) Each character incarnates a certain spiritual attitude toward life and the universe.

In the person of Coeuvre, Marcel tells us that Claudel finds and reincarnates the ancient *vates*, considered in what would have to be its oracular function. Certainly, Victor Hugo also pretended to that prophetic dignity, but lacking a coherent thought and above all an authentic faith, Marcel is convinced that his pretension was only that: a pretension without substance. With Claudel, on the contrary, no doubt is possible; the substance is recuperated, and this is so, Marcel asserts, because of conversion. It is through conversion and only through it that the poet, undoubtedly one of the greatest of all times, found himself as though he were placed at the axis of a truth which is the Truth, that is to say not at all an abstraction, as it could be for Victor Hugo, but the Word, the incarnated Word. Under these condition, there will be nothing surprising in the fact that Coeuvre winds up affirming himself as bishop, a priest among all men. (*Reg* 27-28)

The fact that Claudel is essentially a convert is then profoundly significant for Marcel and he asks if the dramatic work does not appear as an irradiation of conversion, understood as an event that concerns the subject affected to his depths. (*Tr* 69)

Marcel admits that when *The City* was first staged he was among those to whom the attempt seemed daring and undoubtedly destined to failure. But he was also the first to be subjugated by the dramatic power of *The City*. Despite the fact that all theatrical conventions are almost aggressively ignored in the play, Marcel recounts that when listening to it one felt that one was in the presence of a work that was not only brilliant but also prophetic. (*Tr* 18-19)

Similarly, when *Tête d'Or* was created by Jean-Louis Barrault in the Théâtre de France in 1959, Marcel wrote that it represented a phenomenon of which one could find few examples in literary history. It was a work that certainly inspired enthusiasms in some notable writers when it first appeared, but, by and large, it remained ignored during years. It only found its real audience more than 60 years after its appearance among men who were the same age as Claudel when he wrote it. This fact seems even more extraordinary when one thinks of the complete upheaval that took place in the interval. It is only conceivable, remarks Marcel, because in reality *Tête d'Or*, like *The City*, is endowed with a prophetic power. (*Reg* 17-18) He points particularly to the prodigious scene in Part I that culminates in the hymn to the tree; it announced, he tells us, all of French existential philosophy. (*Reg* 164) For Marcel, Claudel is then, in a sense, the father of French existentialism.

Marcel also thought that *L'Échange* (*The Exchange*), like *The City* and *Tête d'Or*, had unfathomable depths in the measure in which it opposes the world of commerce and business to the real world where each being is unique in the very measure that he or she is a creature of God. (*Tr* 23) Finally, there is *Hard Bread*, examined in Chapter 4, one of the harshest works ever conceived, according to Marcel. He describes it as a kind of dramatic exfoliation of Nietzsche's *God is dead*. Yet he acknowledges that it also has a prophetic ring, without any particular event being precisely announced in it. Did we know, he asks, in 1913 when the play was begun, what would happen in our country? (*Reg* 66)

Clearly the linking of this remarkable prophetic quality with conversion and the dramatic work would be unthinkable if conversion were only a psychological event as a certain religious psychology has believed. On the contrary, affirms Marcel, himself a convert; as a result of his conversion Claudel literally entered a universe which had previously been closed to him. This, Marcel tells us, is perfectly discernable in Claudel's first dramatic works, in *Tête d'Or*, but above all in *The City* and in *The Exchange*. (*Tr* 70)

Marcel contends, however, that the freshness, originality and extraordinary emotion that characterize these works, will be lost in Claudel's later works. What was so tragic and at the same time so authentically religious in the early plays will disappear in the later plays. (*Tr* 30-31)

Marcel's critique centers around *Le Soulier de satin* (*The Satin Slipper*). Claudel himself remarks that this entire work is bathed in a feeling of triumph. This feeling of triumph made Marcel think of certain great cupolas of baroque churches, but it also made him very uncomfortable for it seemed to be linked to an exorbitant pretension which was hardly compatible with what he thought were the requirements of a Christian conscience. This pretension consists in daring to place oneself in God's perspective and to consider human beings, here Rodrigue and Prouhèze, the main characters of the play, from God's point of view. The result is that they become like marionettes whose strings God, that is to say here the author, pulls. (*Tr* 30-31)

Let us remember that for Marcel dramatic expression is existential because the characters there are treated as subjects who eventually decides for themselves. The playwright is an artist who creates independent living persons. If, however, these persons are mere mouthpieces or marionettes, then, for Marcel, there is no creation.

Marcel felt that Claudel's triumphalism could much more easily affirm itself in pure lyricism than on the stage. He points out that an enterprise such as *The Satin Slipper* supposes, at its origin, a sort of naivete or ingenuousness completely conceivable in the Middle Ages, that is to say, in an essentially pre-critical or pre-reflective age: it is the fundamental assumption of a work like the *The Divine Comedy*. And, in fact, we know of the admiration that Dante inspired in Claudel. No one would think of considering it unjustified; but Marcel felt that it doesn't at all follow that a twentieth century Dante is possible or even conceivable, and he was not sure that Claudel didn't aspire to be precisely that. (*Tr* 70-72)

Marcel notes that where the poet becomes guilty of presumption, by some sort of mysterious justice, the spectator withdraws. That is what he thinks happens in Act III of *Partage de Midi* (*Break of Noon*) of which Acts I and II are, on the contrary, convincing to the highest degree. He concludes that the sublime—because it is about the sublime—can only be reached where humility is at its height. (*Tr* 86-87) In the course of his career, Marcel found it less and less possible to situate himself at some central point of view which would be like that of God. It seemed to him this would be a pretension completely incompatible with our status as creatures. That is why he always emphasized the importance of humility on the philosophical level, the humility directly opposed to pride, to hubris. He considered it the primordial metaphysical virtue, in opposition to Hegel's panlogical hubris. Naturally, there are difficulties here, because humility can also become pretension and then it is destroyed. But he was convinced—and it is probably in his plays that this is most noticeable—that we simply have to recognize the ambiguity connected with everything that we are insofar as we are equals, subjects. (*R* 252) Very much linked to this is his mistrust of the global and his critique of the idea of totality which perhaps is rather directly related to the one developed by William James in his pluralist period. (*St* 13)   We should recall, too, that the basic characteristic of existential philosophy, at least as Marcel conceived it, was to dispute the validity of the pretensions of totalizing thought.

Curiously enough, it is with the disappearance of the principle of destruction from what he called the Claudelian interior orchestra that he felt the whole of Claudel's opus was damaged. (*Reg* 29)   For him, there was a passage from life—with all its dangers, ambiguities and tragic insecurity—to an effigy of life.

To his mind, at least, Claudel's later work was entirely dominated by a dogmatism completely missing in his early works.   Marcel could not prevent himself from thinking that this dogmatic development, which culminates in *The Satin Slipper*, was somehow linked to Claudel's social ascension, to his becoming an important personage laden with honors and in some way the prisoner of that very importance and of the social comfort to which he acceded. (*Reg* 29)   Marcel was convinced that Claudel paid the ransom for the favors that fortune accorded him. (*Reg* 34)   He thought that Claudel's freshness and originality diminished under the weight of the charges and honors that were to pile up on the shoulders of the public man, of the diplomat.   But he also thought there was a much more intimate and profound reason for this loss.   From the moment when Claudel, definitively installed in a dogmatic Catholicism, saw himself as the spokesperson for that Catholicism, Marcel felt his work lost the extraordinary emotion that still moves audiences so profoundly in his first plays, in particular in *La Jeune Fille Violaine* (*The Girl Violaine*), the first version of *L'Annonce faite à Marie* (*Tidings Brought to Mary*).   (*Tr* 70-71)

Here again we should not forget that Marcel was a watchful philosopher who tried to struggle without pause against a sleep that can affect very different forms at the level of spirit—the sleep of habit, of prejudice, of dogmatism.   He knew that even the authentic religions may become degraded in their very principle of being.   They too can degenerate into idolatries, especially where the will to power is waiting to corrupt them; and this, alas, he felt is almost invariably the case when the Church becomes endowed with temporal authority. (*Mass* 23)

In Marcel's view contestation is fundamental to Christianity today and he felt that unless we voluntarily place ourselves at the level of childhood or of patronage, it is impossible to avoid contestation without betraying the need for truth or producing something like a lifeless pastiche of a medieval mystery. (*Tr* 72-73) We saw how much he admired the voice that announced and exalted the destruction of the established order in *The City*.

For Marcel, the spiritual balance that is desired can in no way present the static character that is discernable in those he called the retired from life. It always presents itself as a precarious victory, let us not say over insecurity itself, but over the anguish that seems to be its almost inevitable consequence. (*St* 300) He prefers questions and tireless movement that ventilates thought to harmonious structure which seems to be satisfied with itself. It was for this reason that he felt closer to Péguy's particular kind of commitment, than to Claudel's, even though he greatly esteemed Claudel's genius and he acknowledged the influence Claudel had on him from 1912-1914.

The many who admire *The Satin Slipper* and who, in fact, consider it Claudel's supreme achievement, will undoubtedly counter this critique by pointing to certain Marcelian traits and insisting that they be taken into account as we consider his assessment of Claudel's contribution.

As Davignon asks, what is one to say of the unfinished aspect of Marcel's own plays where no conclusion is ever given, and of his method characterized by gropings, silences, sinuosities, echoes, modulations, minute and circumspect steps? This method sometimes inspired the feeling of lassitude and inanity even in Marcel who, nevertheless, clearly avowed the importance of it. Perfect agreement was inconceivable for the wayfarer that he was, the itinerant man, the man on his way. For him a person who is no longer on his way is no longer a person. Concluding is not only closing, it is abolishing. (*Mal* 154) We hear him assert that the very notion of a result is a philosophically suspect category. (*PGM* 2) Philosophical research was always an open quest, a search. Even the unalterable and the unconditional encountered in the universal was to be taken as a direction for a journey, not as a resting place. And as Jolin points out, since it is after all the achievement of the universal which makes a wise man, a sage, we can see why Marcel insists that one is not a sage, but is rather always *becoming* a sage (*R* xxix) and why he rejects the Claudel who had *become* an important personage, and *The Satin Slipper*, the play in which Claudel finally succeeded in attaining an interior equilibrium.

CHAPTER 8

CONCLUSION

The Prophetic Phenomenon

To conclude this study, I would like to return to the remarkable assertions made by Marcel that Claudel's early plays, those with a tragic dimension, are prophetic. An examination of this prophetic phenomenon will lead us back to one of the central themes of our exploration: the desire for rational mastery, the will to power, and its relation to inspiration and creativity. In other words, to conclude we will revisit Plato's banishment of the poets.

Yehouda Moraly of Hebrew University in Jerusalem begins his study, "Claudel Voyant" ("Claudel the Seer"), with these three very provocative quotes from Claudel:

The very name of poet among the Latins was that of prophet, *vates*. But poetic inspiration itself is only the accentuation of a general phenomenon. It all happens as though there were no living man, much less woman, who didn't have, sitting on his shoulder, an invisible genie who whispers ideas and promptings to him. It isn't only prophets who are inspired. A philosopher (Bergson), a military man, a financier, a biologist (Claude Bernard), an explorer, a mother, a wife, each one at an important moment in his or her life, whether rarely or often, good or bad, has received a secret inspiration, foreign to the logic and the prevailing opinions of the time. What is one to say of the mystics? What is one to say of the prophets of the Old Testament and of those of the New, whose tradition has continued uninterrupted to our times? The gift of prophecy being moreover clearly distinct from the moral value of its beneficiary, as the case of Caiphas proves, and that, clearer still, of Balaam. To this mysterious gift theology gives a name, that of grace, and it distinguishes two types of grace, *gratia gratis data*, or charism which produces poets, Arthur Rimbaud, for example and *gratia gratum faciens*, that produces saints. (*Opr* 54)

The Artist is the contemporary of his whole life. The events of which he does not have the recollection, he has the presentiment. (*Opr* 284)

Strange words resonate in us like doors? (*Th*, I, 53)[1]

It was not only Marcel then who discerned this prophetic quality in Claudel. Claudel himself reflected on this mystery; we saw as much in Chapter 2.

In his article, Moraly examines four plays written in Claudel's youth, two that Marcel commented on, *The City* and *Tête d'Or*, and two which reflect Claudel's personal story, *Une Mort prématurée* (*A Premature Death*) and *La Jeune Fille Violaine* (*The Girl Violaine*). He points to the fact that these last two plays announce events in Claudel's life many years before they occur. Whereas I certainly do not dispute these conclusions, some of which are corroborated by Claudel's own commentaries and some of which I studied myself in previous work on Claudel,[2] I feel that in the realm of the personal it can always be claimed that what we are dealing with are self-fulfilling prophecies. The case of *Tête d'Or*, on the other hand, is more interesting. Here Moraly claims we have an anticipation of Hitler's adventure. He feels his claim is corroborated by the fact that during the German occupation of France in World War II the collaborationist authorities asked Claudel for the rights to this play. To further substantiate his assertion he points to Tête d'Or's force, to his contempt for what force

---

[1]Cited in Yehouda Moraly "Claudel Voyant" in *Bulletin de la Société Paul Claudel* 139 (1995): 6. Translation mine. Henceforth cited as *CV*.

[2]See B.

can crush, and to his hypnotic sway over the people whose shame is washed and to whom honor and the courage to fight are restored. (*CV* 11) Moraly is convinced that Nazism is clearly a caricature of *Tête d'Or*.

In *The City* Moraly detects the second great phenomenon that marked the twentieth century: the advent of communism, its recent downfall, and the spiritual renewal which is now occurring in the former Soviet Union. It is in the third act of this play that the evocation of the tyrannical regime appears. What follows, however, is an unexpected event. Suddenly, with no warning, the tyrant decides to abandon power. The regime which seemed so solid, founded on terror, will not be swept away by a revolution but will instead be annihilated by its own leader. Clearly, the same sequence of events has taken place in twentieth century Russia. A popular revolution was transformed into a tyrannical dictatorship which threatened the whole world. Then with no war, the regime collapsed slowly from within. There was no opposition from without but rather an absolute metamorphosis begun by the dictator himself. Moraly finds no precedent for this in history, yet it is appears in *The City*. In 1891 Claudel already dreamt of a popular revolution and the relinquishing of power by the dictator himself.

But the last surprise is the most unexpected. After the departure of the dictator, church bells ring in a land where religion officially no longer existed. Contrary to all that could be foreseen, the new regime would be spiritual and religious. Moraly affirms that the former Soviet Union reserved that same surprise for us. The throngs of men and women deprived for years of all spirituality, are rushing to all forms of religion. Russia is becoming an extraordinary center of spiritual renewal.   And this metamorphosis appears in Claudel's 1891 text. (*CV* 12-15)

How are we to account for this prophetic phenomenon which, as we saw, Claudel claims is actually commonplace? (Don't we all know what it is to receive an inspiration?)

René Girard begins his account of the prophetic by noting that we project on literary works—in this case, on novels—the meanings we already project on the world. That projection becomes easier as time passes because the work is "in advance" of a society that only catches up with it slowly. According to Girard, the explanation of this advance has nothing mysterious about it. The novelist is above all the one with the most intense desire. His desire draws him to the most abstract regions and the most meaningless objects. His desire draws him then, almost automatically, toward the summit of the social structure. There, Girard tells us, ontological disease is always the most acute. The symptoms that the novelist observes will propagate themselves slowly toward the lower levels of that society. The metaphysical situations which are represented in the works will become familiar to a great number of readers; the oppositions in the novels will have their exact replica in daily existence. The novelist who reveals the desire of the social elite is then almost always prophetic. He describes intersubjective structures that will slowly become commonplace.[3]

These observations are undoubtedly valid; they in some ways echo Ricoeur's views mentioned in Chapter 3. Ricoeur noted that the emphasis in works of art is on disclosure; they tend to be prospective symbols of personal synthesis and of the future and not merely a regressive symptom of the artist's unresolved conflicts. (*Fr* 521) Yet these observations do not account for the phenomenon of inspiration which Claudel describes and to which Mark Edmundson seems to allude when he says that poems get out ahead of us, creating fresh prospects, new hope. On the other hand, he notes that theory interests itself in the past, in what is already known. Poetry would create the future.[4]

Marcel, too, speaks of this tension between the prophet and the philosopher. He says that the philosopher cannot help feeling in sympathy with the genuine prophet, but at the same time this sympathy is always of an anguished sort, for the very reason that prophecy is always like lightning, flashing transversely across the hard and twisty paths along which the philosopher must grope his way. This prophetic foreshortening

---

[3]René Girard, *Mensonge romantique et vérité romanesque* (Paris: Grasset, 1961), 229. Translation min Henceforth cited as *Mr*.

[4]Mark Edmundson, *Literature Against Philosophy, Plato to Derrida* (Cambridge: Cambridge University Pres 1995), 51. Henceforth cited as *LP*.

frightens the philosopher just because of the infinite danger of distortion it implies.

And with this, we encounter once again the fear that inspired Plato's banishment of the poets and the silencing of the gods. Characteristically, however, Marcel finds that this infinite danger has something positive and one might say necessary about it. (*Mass* 130) Marcel, we must not forget, was both philosopher and playwright. As we have seen, art and music were the underground streams that fed his thought.

But there are also other dimensions to these tensions. We should not forget what Adriaan Peperzak calls philosophy's desire for absolute knowledge which is a desire to conceptually possess and master the universe from an absolute standpoint, the standpoint of an unshaken and unconquerable Ego.[5] In even broader terms, it is, as Girard would have it, always about convincing others, and above all of convincing oneself, that one is perfectly and divinely autonomous. (*Mr* 270-71) The Cartesian ego, *res cogitans*, or mind, is a punctual, highly self-transparent, self-knowing, absolutely unclouded, unoccluded, inertia-free consciousness.[6] Hegel's project is about Spirit struggling to overcome all opposition by transforming every shape of otherness into "its own" or into "its own other." Mark Taylor tells us that the sublation of otherness, be that other religious, psychological, or sociopolitical, is the consistent aim of the modern philosophy of the subject. Hegel's entire philosophy is constructed to dominate, master, and repress otherness. Absolute knowledge is total self-consciousness, which Hegel describes as pure self-recognition in absolute otherness. When other mirrors self, difference is mastered and the subject appears to come into full possession of its proper identity. Taylor notes that such masterful self-possession marks the end, that is, the *telos*, as well as the conclusion, of western philosophy and history.[7]

---

[5]Adriaan T. Peperzak, "Judaism and Philosophy in Lévinas," *Journal for Philosophy of Religion* 40 (1996): 140.

[6]William James Earle "Religion and Television" in *Lacan and Theological Discourse*, eds. Edith Wyschogrod, David Crownfield, Carl A. Raschke (Albany: State University of New York Press, 1989), 139. Henceforth cited as *LTD*.

[7]Mark C. Taylor, "Refusal of the Bar" in *LTD* 42.

But we must object, with Mark Taylor, that the sublating of all otherness, the mastering of all difference in pure self-consciousness is impossible, if for no other reason, as Lacan points out, than that the unconscious is irreducible and precludes the absolute self-transparency of consciousness. (*LTD* 55)

Lacan is persuaded that the Hegelian project is impossible. Reason can never be expanded sufficiently to integrate the irrational without remainder. The modern philosophy of subjectivity, which culminates in Hegel's analysis of absolute self-consciousness, founders on the irreducible unconscious discovered by Freud. (*LTD* 43) Contrary to Hegel's claim that the I is fully realized (and thus desire satisfied) in complete self-consciousness, Lacan contends that the subject is always incomplete and desire never satisfied. Lacan explains that the formation of the I as it is experienced in psychoanalysis is what led him to oppose any philosophy directly issuing from the *Cogito*. The radical heteronomy that Freud's discovery shows gaping within man can never again be covered over without whatever is used to hide it being profoundly dishonest. (*LTD* 44) The tragic cannot be masked. Heidegger, too, would hold that such a model of truth and knowledge conceals its own temporal, historical, self-subverting features in an illusory quest for mastery of knowledge, of the world, of the Other. (*LTD* 158)

According to Earle, what is not, and cannot be, endorsed is Enlightenment psychology, or optimism about cognitive advance, or the view that impediments to enlightenment are all external. (As we have seen, Marcel said as much.) We know, Earle tells us, (when we are not forgetting it, not backsliding into complacency, not lying to ourselves) that there is plenty of internal inertia, opacity, self-renewing, barely defeasible, obtuseness and that the psyche is a not altogether stable confederation of agents and double agents playing their own games, or actors at cross purposes, of inconsistent voices, or mutually subversive energies. (*LTD* 141) (This all reminds us of Claudel's description of his inner theater analyzed in Chapter 6.)

Girard observes that modern man does not suffer because he refuses to become fully aware of his complete autonomy, he suffers because that awareness, real or imagined, is intolerable to him. We see clearly in the novel that the need for transcendence seeks to be satisfied in the here and now and drags the hero into all sorts of follies. (*Mr* 164) Girard calls the truth that hides itself behind rationalist or romantic abstractions the subterranean. The subterranean is the aggravation of a preexisting evil, it is, in fact, a cancerous proliferation of the metaphysics thought to have been suppressed (*Mr* 261) by those for whom God is the obstacle man encounters on his way to full mastery of himself. It is taken for granted that those who reach a certain stage of emancipation can no longer believe in God; atheism corresponds to the indispensable time of spiritual weaning. (*St* 258) We are then left with what Raschke calls a culture where the Cartesian *cogito* has become in effect an "image of the beast," a duplicate of the divine, a virtual apparition of the transcendental signified.[8] Even for Derrida, God is only ostensibly deceased: He has been displaced into a number of cultural forms, chief among them, reason itself. Derrida, much like the members of the Frankfurt School, contends that Western reason has become a deity in its own right and must be submitted to a debunking critique. (*LP* 78)

Girard notes that the moderns who have stopped worshiping God have also begun to worship each other. But since humans are not adorable, the attempt only generates the low comedy of desire, and characteristically modern forms of disappointment and despair. (*LTD* 147) Let us then not say with Martin Heidegger that the gods have withdrawn. The gods are closer than ever. Girard points out that Proust and Dostoevski don't define our universe by the absence of the sacred, as the philosophers do, but by a perverted and corrupted sacred that slowly poisons the sources of life. (*Mr* 206)

Marcel Raymond observes that following the *philosophe's* critique, it was up to art to satisfy some of the human demands which religion, until then, had succeeded in exorcizing.[9] Poetry, from this point on, tends to become an ethics or some kind of

---

[8]Carl Raschke, "Jacques Lacan and the Magic of Desire: A Post-Structuralist Subscript" in *LTD* 60.

[9]Marcel Raymond, *De Baudelaire au Surréalisme* (Paris: Librairie José Corti, 1963), 11. Henceforth cited as *BS*.

irregular means of metaphysical knowledge; it is formed by a need to "change life" as Rimbaud wanted, to change man and to make him touch being. What is new here is the intention, which slowly emerges, to recapture the obscure forces and to try to surmount the dualism of the ego and the universe. Since the end of the eighteenth century, the rational and positivist conception of the universe and of life has established itself ever more strongly and its constraint on the human spirit has been exercised with growing violence. Because this rational and positivist conception has separated us from the universe and from a part of ourselves, from that part where the forces which are not subject to reason reside (and that at the very moment when Christianity, losing its power over souls, seemed to stop offering a way to personal salvation), it exaggerated to an intolerable degree the natural discord between the totalizing demands of the spirit and the limited existence which was man's lot.

Raymond is convinced that since that time the poets have filled a compensatory function in society in the measure in which they have tried to make of the poetic act a vital operation. If poetry is one of the means which are offered to us to assure communication with what Goethe called the "Mothers," it manifests as such a permanent human vocation. (*BS* 11-12)

But as we have remarked, it is communication with the "Mothers" which is feared. (We noted in Chapter 1 that what is banished and suppressed is indeed perceived to be feminine. And so we see Tête d'Or, Claudel's conquering hero, nail to a tree the only female character in the play.) This realm of the "Mothers" is undoubtedly the creative matrix from which inspiration and that mysterious prophetic quality erupt. Claudel's struggles with his muse, studied in Chapter 2, also graphically depict the tensions we have been considering. We saw that the consequence of his success in resisting his muse was his descent into the subterranean regions Girard describes where the cancerous proliferation of the metaphysics thought to have been suppressed occurs. The poet's desire for complete autonomy clearly resulted in his immersion in the subterranean.

Creativity

Finally, let us consider Kenneth Gallagher's reflections on this creative matrix. For Gallagher creativity is characterized by an absolute freshness which has the appearance of being eternal. Is this not exactly the impression which the authentic creations of music, art, and poetry inspire in us? he asks. The newness of creation does not, however, connote an innovation, but a newness whose essence is to be new and which therefore can never be old. Creation is also the revelation of inexhaustibility, for the new being which wells up in creation does not diminish anything else. It can even be said that creative activity does not take place in spatial time because it participates in the eternity of its product. When our attention is creatively engaged we will say that we did not notice that time has gone by; we have withdrawn into the creative moment which does not have any spatial extent. Here, there is only the present. (*PGM* 85-86)

Another remarkable feature which Gallagher says all creativity has in common is that the categories of giving and receiving are surmounted in it. He explains in this way:

> To receive a guest is to admit another into the zone of my person, to allow him to participate in a reality which is properly mine. At this limit, 'receiving' is indistinguishable from 'giving': I only receive by giving, and in the end, perhaps, by giving myself. This becomes still plainer if we examine artistic activity. Is the artist a giver or receiver? We can show the impossibility of an answer to such a question in more than one way. Take the creative idea. Is this an idea which the artist has and then gives to reality? Hardly....The artist does not know what he is going to do until he does it. With the last stroke of his brush, his conception is fully revealed to him. He receives it from the work to which it has given birth. As Marcel would say, we are in the region where invention and discovery coincide. Has the poet made his poem or discovered it? Both and neither. For both are categories which do

> not apply to a creative process: they are illicit importations from a less
> ultimate realm of being. The poet does not first invent his creative idea,
> and then incarnate it in words; he discovers it by incarnating it. It
> comes to be in the creative process. (*PGM* 87)

Here we again encounter the notion of autonomy. Gallagher explains that inspiration does not mean reception in the sense of passivity, for artists are only inspired insofar as they *act*. Yet in acting, they do not behave as autonomous subjects. They are not in control of their next move. For instance, by no effort of will can the poet bring the next word into being. When we act autonomously, the situation is otherwise: the future is in our control and will occur as we decree. In creation our action is actually neither autonomous nor heteronomous. Gallagher is convinced that, in regard to it, the Stoic distinction between what is in our power and what is not collapses completely. A true work of art testifies to a gift from transcendence, but the reception of the inspiration is itself an act of the subject. It is impossible to break down the creative event into juxtaposed elements, one contributed by the subject, one contributed by being. The work is entirely ours and entirely a gift. To create is then not to *make*: it is not a productive activity whose principle is entirely within the self. (*PGM* 88-89)

All creation is, in fact, as Claudel has taught us, a mutual birth (*co-naissance*). Being is spirit: and spirit is creative communion. The transcendent is not a supreme "thing" but the eternal and absolute thou at the heart of all communion. And Gallagher warns that unless the transcendent is so conceived, we are in danger of falling into idolatry (*PGM* 95), into the low comedy of desire.

We join him in concluding that if anything can, the artistic process ought to tell us that the creative self is not an autonomous subject. (*PGM* 89) The instruction of philosophy and psychoanalysis by tragedy undoubtedly occurs because a true work of art indeed testifies to a gift of transcendence.

BIBLIOGRAPHY

Aeschylus. *The Plays of Aeschylus*. Chicago: Wm. Benton, 1952.

Almansi, R. J. "A Psychoanalytic Study of Sophocles '*Antigone*'". *Psychoanalytic Quarterly* 60 (1991): 69-85.

Aristotle. *The Works of Aristotle*. Chicago: Wm. Benton, 1952.

Balthasar, Hans Urs Von. *La Gloire et la croix*. Paris: Aubier, 1968.

————. *Theo-Drama. Theological Dramatic Theory*, Vol. I, *Prolegomena*. San Francisco: Ignatius Press, 1988.

Berman, Emanuel. "Introduction." *Essential Papers on Literature and Psychoanalysis*. Ed. Emanuel Berman. New York: New York University Press, 1993.

Bertrand, P., "Le Sens du tragique et du destin dans la dialectique hégélienne," *Revue de métaphysique et de morale* 47 (1940): 165-186.

Betsworth, Roger G. *Social Ethics. An Examination of American Moral Traditions*. Louisville: Westminster/John Knox Press, 1990.

Blanchot, Maurice. *Le Livre à venir*. Paris: Gallimard, 1959.

Bloom, Harold. "Poetic Crossing: Rhetoric and Psychology," *The Georgia Review* 30 (1976): 495-526.

Brueck, Katherine T. *The Redemption of Tragedy. The Literary Vision of Simone Weil*. Albany: State University of New York Press, 1995.

Bugliani, Ann. "'O la femme qui est en moi': Paul Claudel et 'La Muse qui est la Grâce.'" *Paul Claudel: les Odes*. Ed. Sergio Villani. Woodbridge, Ont.: Les Editions Albion, 1994.

————. *Women and the Feminine Principle in the Works of Paul Claudel*. Madrid: José Porrúa Turanzas, S.A., 1977.

Claudel, Paul. *Journal*. 2 vols. Bibliothèque de la Pléiade. Paris: Gallimard, 1968-1969.

————. *Mémoires improvisés*. Paris. Gallimard, 1969.

————. *Oeuvre poétique*. Bibliothèque de la Pléiade. Paris: Gallimard, 1967.

————. *Oeuvres complètes*. 29 vols. Paris: Gallimard, 1950-1993.

————. *Oeuvres en prose*. Bibliothèque de la Pléiade. Paris: Gallimard, 1965.

————. *Théâtre*. 2 vols. Bibliothèque de la Pléiade. Paris: Gallimard, 1965- 1967.

Crownfield, David. Ed. *Body/Text in Julia Kristeva. Religion, Women, and Psychoanalysis*. Albany: State University of New York Press, 1992.

Davignon, René. *Le mal chez Gabriel Marcel*. Montréal: Editions Bellarmin, 1985.

Derrida, Jacques. "Plato's Pharmacy." *Dissemination*. Trans. Barbara Johnson. Chicago: University of Chicago Press, 1981.

Earle, William James. "Religion and Television." *Lacan and Theological Discourse.*
    Eds. Edith Wyschogrod, David Crownfield, Carl A. Raschke. Albany: State
    University of New York Press, 1989
Edmundson, Mark. *Literature Against Philosophy, Plato to Derrida.* Cambridge:
    Cambridge University Press, 1995.
Ellul, Jacques. *The Humiliation of the Word.* Grand Rapids: Eerdmans, 1985.
————. *The Subversion of Christianity.* Grand Rapids: Eerdmans, 1986.
Felman, Shoshana. *Jacques Lacan and the Adventure of Insight. Psychoanalysis in
    Contemporary Culture.* Cambridge: Harvard University Press, 1987.
Fessard, Gaston. "Théâtre et mystère." *La Soif.* Gabriel Marcel. Paris: Desclée de
    Brower et Cie, 1938.
Freud, Sigmund. *Moses and Monotheism.* London: The Hogarth Press, 1964.
————. *Psychopathic Characters on the Stage. Complete Works*, Vol. VII.
    London: The Hogarth Press, 1953.
————. "Psychology of Women." *New Introductory Lectures in Psycho-Analysis.*
    Chicago: Wm. Benton, 1952.
————. *Totem and Taboo.* New York: New Republic, 1927.
————. *The Works of Sigmund Freud.* Chicago: Wm. Benton, 1952.
Gallagher, Kenneth T. *The Philosophy of Gabriel Marcel.* New York: Fordham
    University Press, 1962.
Gallop, Jane. *The Daughter's Seduction. Feminism and Psychoanalysis.* Ithaca:
    Cornell University Press, 1982.
Gearhart, Suzanne. *The Interrupted Dialectic. Philosophy, Psychoanalysis, and Their
    Tragic Other.* Baltimore: Johns Hopkins University Press, 1992.
Gellrich, Michelle. *Tragedy and Theory: The Problem of Conflict Since Aristotle.*
    Princeton: Princeton University Press, 1988.
Girard, René. *Critiques dans un souterrain.* Paris: Grasset, 1976.
————. *Des choses cachées depuis la fondation du monde.* Paris: Grasset, 1978.
————. *Mensonge romantique et vérité romanesque.* Paris: Grasset, 1961.
————. *Quand ces choses commenceront....* Paris: Arlea, 1994.
Goethe, Johann Wolfgang von. *Essays on Art and Literature.* New York: Suhrkamp
    Publishers, c1986.
Hart, Kevin. *The Trespass of the Sign.* Cambridge: Cambridge University Press, 1989.
Hegel, G.W.F. *The Philosophy of History.* Chicago: Wm. Benton, 1952.
Heidegger, Martin. *Poetry, Language, Thought.* New York: Harper & Row, 1971.
Irigaray, Luce. *An Ethics of Sexual Difference.* Ithaca: Cornell University Press, 1993.
————. *Le corps-à-corps avec la mère.* Montréal: Les éditions de la pleine lune,
    1981.
————. *Spéculum de l'autre femme.* Paris: Editions de minuit, 1974.
Kant, Emmanuel. *Critique of Practical Reason.* Chicago: Wm. Benton, 1952.
Kojève, Alexandre. *Introduction to the Reading of Hegel.* New York: Basic Books,
    1969.
Kowsar, Mohammad. "Desire and *The Hostage*." *Theatre Journal* 46.1 (March 1993):
    79-93.
————. "Lacan's *Antigone*: A Case Study in Psychoanalytical Ethics." *Critical*

Theory and Performance. Eds. Janelle G. Reinelt and Joseph R. Roach. Ann Arbor: The University of Michigan Press, 1992.

Krieger, Murray, *The Tragic Vision.* New York: Holt, Rinehart and Winston, 1960.

Lacan, Jacques. "Le mythe individuel du névrosé." *Ornicar?* 17/18 (1979): 289-307.

————. *Le Séminaire de Jacques Lacan,* Livre VII, *L'éthique de la psychanalyse.* Paris: Editions du Seuil, 1986.

————. *Le Séminaire de Jacques Lacan,* Livre VIII, *Le Transfert.* Paris: Editions du Seuil, 1991.

————. *The Four Fundamental Concepts of Psycho-analysis.* New York: W. W. Norton & Co., 1978.

————. "The Neurotic's Individual Myth." Trans. Martha Noel Evans. *The Psychoanalytic Quarterly* 48 (1979): 405-25.

Lacey, Michael. "The Backwardness of American Catholicism." *Conversations* 8 (Fall 1995): 9.

Lacoue-Labarthe, "La Scène est primitive," *Le Sujet de la philosophie. Typographies I.* Paris: Aubier-Flammarion, 1979.

Lee, Jonathan Scott. *Lacques Lacan.* Amherst: The University of Massachusetts Press, 1990.

Lévinas, Emmanuel. *Entre Nous.* Paris: Grasset, 1991.

Lubac, Henri de. *Theological Fragments.* San Francisco: Ignatius Press, 1989.

Lyotard, Jean-François, "The Sublime and the Avant-Garde,"*Artforum* 40 (April 1984): 36-43.

MacIntyre, Alasdair. *After Virtue.* South Bend: Notre Dame University Press, 1984.

Marcel, Gabriel. *Du refus à l'invocation.* Paris: Gallimard, 1940.

————. *Etre et avoir.* Paris: Aubier, 1935.

————. *Homo viator.* Paris: Aubier, 1945.

————. "Influence du Théâtre," *Revue des jeunes* (March 5, 1935): 349-362.

————. *Journal Metaphysique.* Paris: Gallimard, 1927.

————. *Le mystère de l'être.* I & II. Paris: Aubier, 1951.

————. *Man Against Mass Society.* Lanham: University Press of America, 1985.

————. *Philosophy of Existence.* Plainview, N.Y.: Books for Libraries Press, 1969.

————. *Positions et approches concrètes du mystère ontologique.* Paris: Vrin, 1949.

————. *Pour une sagesse tragique et son au-delà.* Paris: Plon, 1968

————. *Regards sur le théâtre de Claudel.* Paris: Beauchesne, 1964.

————. *Théâtre et religion.* Lyon: Editions Emmanuel Vitte, 1958.

————. "The Drama of the Soul in Exile" in *Three Plays.* London: Secker & Warburg, 1952.

————. *The Existential Background of Human Dignity.* Cambridge: Harvard University Press, 1963.

————. *Tragic Wisdom and Beyond Including Conversations Between Paul Ricoeur and Gabriel Marcel.* Evanston: Northwestern University Press, 1973.

McKenna, Andrew. *Violence and Difference.* Urbana: University of Illinois Press, 1992.

Miceli, Vincent P. *Ascent to Being.* Foreword by Gabriel Marcel. New York: Desclee

Company, 1965.

Mill, John Stuart. *Bentham*. Chicago: Encyclopedia Britannica, Inc., 1993.

————. *Utilitarianism*. Chicago: Wm. Benton, 1952.

Moraly, Yehouda. "Claudel Voyant." *Bulletin de la Société Paul Claudel* 139 (1995): 6-20.

Moran, Denis P. *Gabriel Marcel*. Lanham, Md.: University Press of America, 1984.

Neuringer, Charles. "Freud and Theatre." *Journal of the American Academy of Psychoanalysis* 20.1 (Spring 1992): 142-128.

Nussbaum, Martha C. *The Fragility of Goodness. Luck and Ethics in Greek Tragedy and Philosophy*. Cambridge: Cambridge University Press, 1986.

Peperzak, Adriaan T. "Judaism and philosophy in Levinas." *International Journal for Philosophy of Religion* 40 (December 1996): 125-145.

Plato. *The Dialogues of Plato*. Chicago: Wm. Benton, 1952.

Raschke, Carl. "Jacques Lacan and the Magic of Desire: A Post-Structuralist Subscript." *Lacan and Theological Discourse*. Eds. Edith Wyschogrod, David Crownfield, Carl A. Raschke. Albany: State University of New York Press, 1989

Raymond, Marcel. *De Baudelaire au Surréalisme*. Paris: Librairie José Corti, 1963.

Richardson, William. "Love and the Beginning." *Contemporary Psychoanalysis*. 28.3 (July 1992): 423-442.

Ricoeur, Paul. *A Ricoeur Reader: Reflection and Imagination*. Ed. MarioValdés. Toronto: University of Toronto Press.

————. *Entretiens: Paul Ricoeur et Gabriel Marcel*. Paris: Aubier-Montaigne, 1968.

————. *Freud and Philosophy: An Essay on Interpretation*. Trans. Denis Savage. New Haven: Yale University Press, 1970.

————. *Gabriel Marcel et Karl Jaspers*. Paris: Temps présent, 1948.

————. *Oneself as Another*. Trans. Kathleen Blamey. Chicago: University of Chicago Press, 1992.

————. *The Symbolism of Evil*. Trans. Emerson Buchanan. New York: Harper and Row, 1967.

Rohde, Erwin. *Psyche*. New York: Harper and Row, 1966.

Sallis, John. *Crossings: Nietzsche and the Space of Tragedy*. Chicago: University of Chicago Press, 1991.

Scheler, Max. *Le phénomène du tragique*. Paris: Aubier, 1952.

Schindler, David L. Ed. *Hans Urs von Balthasar: His Life and Work*. San Francisco: Ignatius Press, 1991.

Simon, B. *Tragic drama and the family: Pschoanalytic studies from Aeschylus to Beckett*. New Haven and London: Yale University Press, 1988.

Sophocles. *The Plays of Sophocles*. Chicago: Wm. Benton, 1952.

Szondi, Peter. *A Theory of Modern Drama*. Minneapolis: University of Minnesota Press, 1987.

————. *On Textual Understanding and Other Essays*. Minneapolis: University of Minnesota Press, 1986.

Taylor, Mark. "Refusal of the Bar." *Lacan and Theological Discourse*. Eds Edith

Wyschogrod, David Crownfield, Carl A. Raschke. Albany: State University of New York Press, 1989

Tilliette, Xavier. *Philosophes contemporains*. Paris: Desclée de Brouwer, 1962.

Troisfontaines, Roger. *De l'existence à l'être*, I & II. Paris: J. Vrin, 1953.

Vernant, J.P. "Ambiguity and Reversal: On the Enigmatic Structure of *Oedipus Rex*." *New Literary History* 10.3 (1978): 491-92.

————. *Myth and Thought Among the Greeks*. Boston: Routledge and Kegan Paul, 1983.

Wahl, Jean. *Vers le concret*. Paris: J. Vrin, 1932.

Werman, David, "Methodological Problems in the Psychoanalytic Interpretation of Literature: A Review of Studies on Sophocles' *Antigone*." *Essential Papers on Literature and Psychoanalysis*. Ed. Emmanuel Berman. New York: New York University Press, 1993: 217-237.

White, David A. *Heidegger and the Language of Poetry*. Lincoln: University of Nebraska Press, 1978.

Wyschogrod, Edith, et al. Eds. *Lacan and Theological Discourse*. Albany: State Univerity of New York Press, 1989.

Zizek, Slavoj. "Philosophy Traversed by Psychoanalysis," *Textual Practice*, 6.3 (Winter 1992): 402-420.

INDEX